ASSEMBLE TOGETHER

*A book of assemblies
for middle and secondary schools*

by
TONY CASTLE

GEOFFREY CHAPMAN
LONDON

A Geoffrey Chapman book published by
CASSELL LTD.
35 Red Lion Square, London WC1R 4SG
and at Sydney and Toronto

an affiliate of Macmillan Publishing Co. Inc.,
New York

First published 1981

British Library Cataloguing in Publication Data
Castle, Tony
    Assemble together.
    1. Worship programmes
    I. Title
    377'.1   BV283.S3

I.S.B.N. 0 225 66296 5

Typeset by Inforum Ltd., Portsmouth.
Printed in Great Britain by
Richard Clay (The Chaucer Press) Ltd,
Bungay, Suffolk

Dedicated to Sister Mary Pius
and all the pupils, past and present,
of St Thomas Becket School, Abbey Wood.

Introduction

The material assembled together in this book is structured in such a way as to be of use on a variety of occasions and under varying conditions.

The sixty 'Prepared Assemblies' make use of pop music, as well as classical music, role-play and posters together with lively readings and prayers. These may be used just as they are presented, or, better still, may be adapted for local use. The second set, sixty 'Alternative Assemblies', are more formal and traditional in form and content.

The assemblies in the first part are arranged in Sections A–G. Each section has a different content slant. Section A (A1–A10) develops the concept of 'community'; it is more open-ended than most of the others, offering the possibility of further development in the classroom. Section B (B11–B20) consists of explicitly Christian material centred around the Christian festivals of Christmas, Easter and Whitsun. Five assemblies comprise Section C (C21–C25): written around an allegory, they can be used either on successive days of the same week or over a period of five weeks. The allegory develops some of the basic themes of Christianity, so these assemblies are explicitly Christian in content. Section D (D26–D35) is based upon Old Testament heroes; the beliefs and customs of the major world religions appear in the themes selected for Section E (E36–E45). The central theme of F (F46–F50) is the family and the content is only implicitly Christian. This is another section that would benefit from follow-up development in class. The last section, G (G51–G60) is composed of a selection of explicitly Christian themes of interest and value to young people.

The more traditional and formal assembly programmes in 'Alternative Assemblies' generally follow the themes and usually the same titles as the corresponding 'Prepared Assemblies'. This makes it possible to use texts from 'Prepared Assemblies' in 'Alternative Assemblies', and vice-versa.

Listed in the Indexes will be found all the hymns and songs recommended in the book, together with selections from the realm of pop music. The posters proposed for use in some assemblies are obtainable from Palm Tree Press or Argus Communications; this medium is being rapidly extended and users are recommended to write to the publishers concerned for up-to-date catalogues – Palm Tree Press is at 55 Leigh

Road, Leigh on Sea, Essex; Argus Communications is at DLM House, Edinburgh Way, Harlow, Essex, CM20 2HL.

It is my hope that, after using the fully-worked-out assemblies for a short while, the reader will gain in both enthusiasm and confidence and feel free to use the whole book merely as a resource base for his or her own assembly.

I would like to express my gratitude to the following head teachers and teachers, who offered comments upon the final manuscript and kindly used and experimented with the assembly programmes: Brian Sherratt, Sister Patrick Ignatius, Ann Irwin, Bert White, Mike Coy and Hugh and Andrea McGinley. A special word of thanks to Jacquie Galley for typing, and retyping, the manuscript.

TONY CASTLE
February 1981

Contents

As explained in the Introduction, there are two series of assemblies in this book, 'Prepared Assemblies' and 'Alternative Assemblies'. The two series are parallel and most of the themes are found in both series. For this reason, and to illustrate the structure of the book, the Contents are given in integrated form. Assembly references are printed in bold characters, page numbers in *italic*.

Christian Calling and Life
(*Note:* 'Prepared Assemblies' C21–C25 consist of an allegory, 'Climb the Dark Wall', in five episodes which should be taken consecutively. For individual treatment of the topics listed below, the 'Alternative Assemblies' are to be preferred.)

The Bible — Old Testament

World Religious Themes

Acknowledgements

The author and publishers would like to thank the following for permission to reproduce copyright material:
Associated Book Publishers Ltd for two poems by John Oxenham from *First Prayers for Children*, published by Methuen & Co. Ltd; Associated Catholic Publications Ltd for the poem 'Gold, Frankincense and Myrrh' by Killian Twell OFM from *No Rich Design* and extracts from *52 Talks for Young People* by Maurice Nassan SJ; Associated Newspapers Group Ltd for stories that appeared in *Daily Mail*, London, 'Escape from the Incredible Hulk' by Alun Rees and 'Baboo, a man of peace who was kicked to death' by Tim Miles; Ave Maria Press, Notre Dame, Indiana for an excerpt from *There is a Season* by Eugene S. Geissler, 1969; *Basildon Evening Echo* for 'How I survived the waves of death'; Mrs Rodney Bennett for the poem 'Windy Nights' by Rodney Bennett; Donald Butler for passages from *Many Lights*, published by Geoffrey Chapman, a division of Cassell Ltd; Jonathan Cape Ltd and the executors of the Laurence Housman estate for an extract 'Light looked down' from *Little Plays of Saint Francis* Volume II; Church Information Office for an extract from *Live and Pray* by Brother Kenneth CGA and Sister Geraldine DssCSA; William Collins, Sons & Co. Ltd for two extracts from *Something Beautiful for God* by Malcolm Muggeridge, one passage from *Miracle on the River Kwai* by Ernest Gordon, two prayers by William Barclay from *Prayers for Young People*, for an excerpt from *Incognito* by Petru Dumitriu and from *Autobiography* by Yevtushenko; Darton, Longman & Todd Ltd for two passages from *The Jerusalem Bible* published and copyright 1966, 1967 and 1968 by Darton, Longman & Todd Ltd and Doubleday & Co. Inc.; Doubleday & Co. Inc. for 'Words are the bridges', originally entitled 'The written word', and 'Never let a thought shrivel and die', originally entitled 'The wonderful words', from *Words, Words, Words* by Mary O'Neill, copyright 1966 by Mary O'Neill; Granada Publishing Ltd for the words of 'Dance over the mountains' by M.E. Rose from *The Morning Cockerel Book of Readings*; Harcourt Brace Jovanovich Inc. for 'What kind of liar are you?' from *The People, Yes* by Sandburg; David Higham Associates Ltd for the poem 'How many Heavens' by Edith Sitwell; Hodder & Stoughton Ltd for prayers by Nancy Martin published in *Prayers for Children and Young*

People, 1975, also for an extract from *The Ascent of Everest* by Sir John Hunt, published in 1953, and for material from *Uncommon Prayers for Young People* by Cecil Hunt; Miss Brenda Holloway for a prayer from *Prayers for Children*, published by Hodder & Stoughton Ltd; Christy Kenneally for the poem 'The Holy Spirit' from the Veritas RE programme; London Associated News and Feature Services for material concerning Naomi James and an article by Clive Hirschorn on Roy Castle; Mayhew-McCrimmon Ltd for the story 'The Cross in the Sand' by the Rev. D.H. Willoughby from *The New Sower*, Winter 1977; A.R. Mowbray & Co. Ltd for passages from *God'll Fix It* by Jimmy Savile OBE; Sister Mary Oswin for the poem 'Where does the wind come from?' published by Mayhew McCrimmon Ltd; Oxford University Press for a selection of passages from Alan Dale's *New World*, copyright Oxford University Press, 1967; Palm Tree Press Ltd for five passages from 'Climb the Dark Wall' by Nigel Sustins in *The Young Christian's Annual*; St Paul Publications for 'Mother Maria' by Frances V. Stantan, from *Meet God and Live*; Penguin Books Ltd for an excerpt from 'The Sumerian Underworld' from *Poems of Heaven and Hell from Ancient Mesopotamia*, trans. by N.K. Sanders, Penguin Classics, 1971; A.D. Peters & Co. Ltd for an excerpt from 'An Only Child' by Frank O'Connor; Mr & Mrs Pole for the use of 'My answer' by Hilary J. Pole; Laurence Pollinger Ltd and the estate of the late Mrs Frieda Lawrence Ravagli for the poem 'Phoenix' by D.H. Lawrence, from *The Complete Poems of D.H. Lawrence*; Rt Revd V. Sanmiguel, bishop of Kuwait, for 'Pastor in Kuwait'; Vallentine, Mitchell & Co. Ltd, for an extract from *The Diary of Anne Frank*; the Rev. Robin J. Williamson for 'The Binmen of Belfast' from *Thought for the Day*.

PREPARED
ASSEMBLIES

The reader is advised to read through the text of an assembly not less than twenty-four hours before use, in order to make any preparations and adaptations required in accordance with local resources.

Community

A1   Community

Introduction
(not to be read) *As the pupils gather for the assembly, a workman (disguised member of staff) is seen to be on the stage (or in the area where the assembly is to take place), absorbed in a maintenance or repair job. When all are gathered, the assembly leader, having called for quiet, approaches the 'workman', who continues his work, oblivious of the presence of anyone else.*

Role-play

ASSEMBLY LEADER
(Aloud for all to hear:) Excuse me, would you mind moving. Perhaps you could come back later and finish what you are doing.

WORKMAN
Sorry, . . . (Miss *or* Sir), I must get this finished now.

ASSEMBLY LEADER
I'm afraid you'll have to go – we are just about to start assembly.

WORKMAN
What's assembly?

ASSEMBLY LEADER
Well, it's when we all *(adapt as necessary)* get together as a community to think about things and gather our thoughts for the day.

WORKMAN
What's a community?

At this point, four or five pupils, one at a time, walk on to the stage (assembly area) and say out loud, 'I'm me.' When the last has arrived, they join hands and say together, 'We're us.' They sit down where they are and immediately five more come in, carrying posters or placards. The first has the word 'Family' on it; coming to the centre, the pupil carrying it says, 'A family is a community.' Next comes a card reading 'Neighbourhood' and the pupil says, 'The neighbourhood can be a community.' There follows

'Club' and 'Class' with 'A . . . is a community.' Last comes 'School', when the pupil carrying this placard joins the others, standing in a line facing the assembled pupils. All together, they say, 'The school is a community.'

Record

(This is turned up as the placard-bearers sit down.) 'Grandma's party tonight', Paul Nicholas, RSO 2090 216 *(fade after a short time).*

Assembly Leader's Comments

Why do we go to parties? To have a good time? To meet our friends? Just to be with a crowd? One thing is certain – you can't have a party just by yourself.

Reading

Len Steels, rugged and grey, gathered sobbing men and women into his arms and asked pathetically, 'What can a man say? What can a man do?' He couldn't cry. Not even when they told him he had lost ten members of his family, including four sons.

Scaffolding inside a cooling tower at a new power station in West Virginia, USA, unwound like apple peel, plunging them and 41 others to their deaths. Len, 54, who has battled against cancer for ten years, could hardly bear the grief shared by the little hamlet of Cow Creek, where all his family lived.

Local Police Sergeant Mike Comer said it all: 'This is a close community, where just about everybody is related. When one feels pain, we all feel pain.'

'Four boys – I lost four boys,' said Len. 'We was very close, me and my sons. I trust in God. He'll never put more on me than I can bear. He gets me through the rough spots. But Lord, it's hard.'

Only minutes before, he had stood, disbelieving, outside a makeshift morgue set up at the tiny fire station at Belmont, West Virginia.

Yesterday, he tried to draw comfort from his only surviving son, Robert, 35, who had been working nearby when the top of the cooling tower at Pleasant Power Station in the town of St Mary's suddenly collapsed.

Comment

A community is a group of people that share both good and bad times together.

(If a hymn or prayer is desired, turn to Alternative Assembly 1.)

A2   Need for One Another

Opening record   'He is your brother', Abba, *Greatest Hits (fade after 1 min. 20 sec.).*

Comment   The words, 'treat him well he is your brother', 'we depend on one another' come across very strongly. Not long ago there was a strike by lorry drivers. We know that if, for example, doctors go on strike, the community is hit very hard, but until the lorry drivers went on strike very few people had even noticed them. Their strike nearly ruined us all, because for the first time we realised how much we depend on lorry drivers to move all the things we need around the country. We depend on one another and working together makes life easier and happier.

Reading   A blind man and a lame man happened to come at the same time to a piece of very bad road. The former begged the latter to guide him through his difficulties. 'How can I do that', said the lame man, 'as I am scarcely able to drag myself along? But if you were to carry me I can warn you about anything in the way; my eyes will be your eyes and your feet will be mine.' 'With all my heart,' replied the blind man, 'let us serve one another.' So taking his lame companion on his back they travelled in this way with safety and pleasure.

Aesop's Fables

Role-play   *A group of pupils (five to eight in number) wander on to the stage or assembly area, chatting quietly among themselves. They stand in a circle facing one another. A lone pupil enters, sees the group and quickly hurries away in another direction. A second pupil enters and walks confidently up to the group. He says, 'Hello' and the group ignore him, closing up their ranks. He tries again and their indifference becomes hostile. He moves off. The group dissolves and withdraws.*

Record   'He is your brother' *(as above): volume turned up as group dissolves. Finish off the track.*

Comment	(*Showing poster* PT 9) People are lonely because they build walls instead of bridges! Some people make no effort to join in and become lonely, others try and are rejected. We must erect no walls to exclude others and be bridge-builders instead.
	(*If a hymn or prayer is desired, turn to* Alternative Assembly 2.)

A3   Communication

Record	*Theme music from Star Wars, Doctor Who or Star Trek (fade).*
Comment	Communication between astronauts and ground-control is essential. Without it no space mission would be possible. Imagine what it would be like to be way out in space with no contact with earth. Naomi James, the young woman who sailed round the world on her own, in a yacht, discovered what it was like. She tried to contact her husband Rob and failed.
Reading	Some time after leaving the Canaries I began to lose track of time. Although I wrote the date each day in my ship's log, I wasn't aware of days in the usual sense; there was nothing to distinguish Thursday from Sunday, for example. I could expect no human contact (except via the radio) for the next two-and-a-half months when there would be a rendezvous off Cape Town.
	I passed the Cape Verde Islands on 4 October (day 26) and the following day put through a call to Rob's father to find out if Rob had reached Cape Town. I learned that he was due to arrive next day.
	So on day 28, I phoned Rob's father again. He told me he had spoken to his son only five minutes previously and gave me the number to ring that evening. I was thrilled to think I would soon be talking to Rob.
	I made notes of the things I wanted to talk to Rob about and fiddled away until the time when he would be expecting the call.

There had been delays on some previous calls. So, I put up the aerial and turned on the set some two hours before Rob was expecting me. I was ready to go, but when I picked up the handset to make the call – nothing happened.

I stared at the radio for a minute, thinking there must have been something I'd forgotten to do, but no, everything seemed to be in order and still the radio remained dead.

An hour later, I had a sick and desperate feeling. I'd done everything I could and had no idea what to do next, I couldn't believe it was a major fault; it just couldn't be, I kept telling myself. I'd found all the radio spares and changed some fuses, but to no avail.

I washed the deck terminal with fresh water and even got out the instruction manual – I might as well have tried to learn Greek in one sitting. I even looked inside the radio, but that was so alarming I shut it again quickly.

The thought of Rob waiting for my call that night, and perhaps for the next four weeks, made me feel quite desperate. I racked by brains to see if there was something I'd overlooked, but there was nothing.

I sat in utter dejection, till I knew Rob would have given up waiting for my call. He would presume I'd not been able to get through and would wait again tomorrow. . . .

Slowly it dawned on me that I still had thousands of miles to go to Cape Town and unless I could hail a passing ship no one would know if I were alive or dead.

For my own part I never expected help to come from the radio, but I hated more than anything else not being able to relieve the anxiety of my family, who would now be faced with total silence.

Naomi James

Comment   We've all met Buzby – the little cheery bird who tells us, on TV and posters, to make someone happy with a phone call. How true that is. If there's good news we can share the joy, if there's a friend in trouble we can offer to help. Being able to communicate is all impor-

tant. But the power of speech also brings responsibilities. Listen to these words of wisdom from famous
writers.

READER A   Nature has given to man one tongue, but two ears, that
we may hear from others as much as we speak.

Epictetus

Comment   That emphasises the importance of learning to listen
well to others; it's a selfish person who 'hogs' all the
conversation.

READER B   There are few wild beasts more to be dreaded than a
talking man having nothing to say.

Jonathan Swift

Comment   There's a saying that 'empty vessels make the most
noise'. That can be true and 'gossip' often harms
others.

READER C   Gossip, unlike river water, flows both ways.

Michael Korda

Comment   If you tell tales about others, remember they too will
certainly gossip about you, when you are not there.

READER D   Conversation is the image of the mind. As a man is, so is
his talk.

Publilius Syrus

Comment   What we say and how we say it, shows others what we
are really like inside. Let us close with these words
(showing the poster).

Poster   (*See* PT 21)
A wise old owl sat on an oak.
The more he saw the less he spoke;
The less he spoke the more he heard.
Why aren't we like that wise old bird?

A4   Truth-telling

Opening record   Tchaikovsky's *1812 Overture*, op. 49, finale (*last 1½ min., fade*).

Comment   The following reading is of a true event which took place in the Second World War, when the Russian armies were storming Berlin – the final moments of the war.

Reading 1   'Get out, get out', the old man cried. 'Get out, run for your lives. The SS have explosives in the cellar, get out.' The half-crazed caretaker's cries were totally ignored. No one believed him. Women and children poured into the once-smart departmental store to plunder what they could. In the distance the rumble of the Russian guns was getting ever nearer.

The caretaker abandoned his post at one of the doors – the hordes of plunderers had swarmed in the other doors and smashed the shop windows – and hobbled out to an old cycle. Without another look over his shoulder he cycled off as fast as he could.

Not two minutes after he had disappeared from view, while hundreds of desperate scavengers hunted for food and clothing, the floor of the store erupted in a tremendous earthquaking explosion. No one in the building stood a chance. In a second or two floors went up and walls caved in. The explosives stored by the SS in the cellar had been detonated by a time bomb. Over 300 women and children died because they did not accept the truth of what the caretaker had told them.

Anon.

Comment   Truth is not always easy to listen to – especially when it doesn't seem to be to our advantage. Nor is it always easy to speak the truth. Think about these proverbs from around the world.

READER A   From France: 'Individuals may perish, but truth is eternal.'

(*Pause between readings*)

READER B	From India: 'The name of God is truth.'
READER C	From Yugoslavia: 'Tell the truth and run.'
READER D	From Israel: 'A half truth is a whole lie.'
Comment	We are social beings; we are beings that need others. We need good happy relationships, but these cannot be built unless there is trust between people. Relationships can only be built if the truth is told.
Reading 2	Real growth in art and life comes to us from the outside as well as from within, comes to us from our relationships with other things and other people. It does not come to us from within or from without, but from within and without at the same time, so that we must always be building bridges. Without bridges we go nowhere.

Eugene S. Geissler, 'The heart has its seasons'

| *Closing record* | Tchaikovsky's *1812 Overture*, finale *(opening minute, fade)*. |

A5   Personal Responsibility

Opening record 'Eye-level', Simon Park, Columbia DB 8946.

Eight pupils sit on the stage, or assembly area, and after 30 seconds of the record stand in a line facing the assembled gathering. The first, third, fifth and seventh remain standing while the others, spaced between them, bend their knees in a squatting position. then in time to the beat of the music and perfectly in unison (a practice will of course be necessary) with their companions they go up and down like a line of pistons. They stop when the music is faded.

Comment   We are not machines or puppets. We are human beings with free will. We do not move all the time like a line of pistons in a car engine or puppets on strings. What we do we are responsible for — whether it is good or bad.

Reading 1

'Escape from the incredible hulk.' It looked as if Doreen Smalley's last moment had come when the incredible hulk dropped in. 'I was playing patience when I heard this low rumbling noise', she said yesterday. 'I looked out of the window and just couldn't believe my eyes. I saw what looked like a big tank coming towards the house. It hit the house with a tremendous bang.'

In fact it was a 12ft high 20 ton runaway mechanical digger which had been set on a backwards destructive path by a group of young vandals who by-passed 'stop' devices with two bent nails.

The digger started its trail of destruction a quarter of a mile away at a council compound in Bolton Road. It crossed three roads . . . demolished heavy iron fencing, trees and a lamp standard . . . then ploughed over an allotment before crashing to a halt against Mrs Smalley's home.

Damage is estimated at £20,000. Mrs Smalley's husband, Albert, who was on night shift at the time, reckoned yesterday that £15,000 of that damage was caused to the house.

He said: 'It looks as if the house will have to be demolished.'

Mr Gordon Brown, the contractor who owns the digger, said: 'Somehow the vandals managed to by-pass the immobilisation system. It's fantastic how the machine managed to travel so far, but these things are just like tanks.'

Last night, West Yorkshire police said they were anxious to trace four boys seen running from the council compound. They are believed to be aged around 9 to 12.

Daily Mail

Comment

When the boys just mentioned were caught, it would be untrue for them to say, 'It's not my fault' or 'You're always picking on me.' They deliberately did something which resulted in the destruction of a house. The owner of the digger said, 'Somehow the vandals managed to by-pass the immobilisation system'. To be mature and grown up we must learn to accept responsibility for what we do.

Reading 2   Here is a maturity check-list. How do you rate?

A Maturity Check-up

1 A mature person does not take himself too seriously – his job, yes!
2 A mature person keeps himself alert in mind.
3 A mature person does not always 'view with alarm' every adverse situation that arises.
4 A mature person is too big to be little.
5 A mature person has faith in himself which becomes stronger as it is fortified by his faith in God.
6 A mature person never feels too great to do the little things and never too proud to do the humble things.
7 A mature person never accepts either success or failure in themselves as permanent.
8 A mature person never accepts any one of his moods as permanent.
9 A mature person is one who is able to control his impulses.
10 A mature person is not afraid to make mistakes.

Leonard Wedel

Record   *Replay opening record.*

A6   Respect for Self

Opening record 'Building my body', Don McLean, *Prime Time*, EMI NS 3011.

Role-play   *Three members of staff are needed; if they can make any of the following statements (or similar ones) truthfully so much the better. Standing where they can be clearly seen and heard they make their comments.*

STAFF ONE   I'm slimming – with my new diet I lost nearly ten ounces last week.

STAFF TWO   I go for a jog every morning – it makes me feel really fit.

STAFF THREE   I gave up smoking last month – now I can really taste the flavour of food.

Comment   People diet to keep fit – run or jog to keep trim – give up smoking to take care of their health. It is very important to look after our bodies – we have only got one and we will never have another! Can you imagine life without being able to run and play games? Worse still being unable to move a muscle and not even being able to see? Hilary Pole was such a person.

Reading 1   Hilary started life just like any other child, healthy and strong. She grew up to be very good at games and dancing. She became a PE and dance teacher. Then quite suddenly a terrible disease struck. Hilary could feel and hear everything, but she couldn't move. She couldn't move her hands or her feet, her arms or her legs. She couldn't move her mouth or her eyelids. She couldn't sing; she couldn't talk; she couldn't make a sound. Because she couldn't chew, or eat, she was fed through tubes and kept alive with a breathing machine.

The only thing she could move was the big toe of her right foot. Her big toe would give a tiny flicker, $1/16$th of an inch, less than 2 mm, when she wanted it to. The only other thing Hilary could do was hear.

But Hilary didn't just give up and die. For ten years she carried on speaking and smiling, praying and helping – through her big toe. At first she had to spell the words out but, after three years, science came to help Hilary and she got a Possum machine. This meant she was able to operate a whole range of switches – turn on the radio, and, most important of all, operate a typewriter. Letters poured from her; she wrote poems and articles. She worked so hard for handicapped people that in 1973 the Queen wrote to her to tell her that she had been awarded the MBE for her brave work for others.

Anon.

Comment   Here is one of Hilary's poems.

Reading 2   *My Answer*

I'm often asked if I am bored,
Frustrated, lonely,
My life abhorred.
And so I answer,
'I am not.' . . .
That now I can accept my lot,
Remind the sadly shaking head
'It is my body, not my mind, in bed.'

I'm rarely frightened or in pain,
For this
I thank my God again.
I have many loyal friends,
My joy in them despair transcends.
There's music too,
Books to read:
Discontentment cannot breed.

Although I can no longer play,
I can listen
Every day
To football, rugby, tennis, cricket,
Imagination has no limit.
Add to this
A sense of humour
Killing that 'depression' rumour.

Now I have my Possum too,
A miracle
In all men's view.
No longer do I have to wait.
My poems and letters to dictate.
Just flick my toe
And type myself,
I have no time to brood on 'health'!

Hilary J. Pole

Closing record   *Repeat part of opening record.*

A7   Respect for Others

Opening record   'He is your brother', Abba, *Greatest Hits*, Epic 69218 *or*
'He ain't heavy, he's my brother', Hollies, Parlophone
R 5806.

Comment   It's easy to turn a brother or sister into an enemy by
unkindness and disrespect. That we must always try
hard to avoid. It is also possible to turn an enemy into a
brother. By respect for him.

Reading 1   In 1941, Mama took me back to Moscow. There I saw
our enemy for the first time. If my memory is right,
nearly 20,000 German war prisoners were to be
marched in a single column through the streets of
Moscow.

The pavements swarmed with onlookers, cordoned
off by soldiers and police. The crowd were mostly
women. Russian women with hands roughened by
hard work, lips untouched by lipstick and thin
hunched shoulders which had borne half the burden of
the war. Every one of them must have had a father or a
husband, or brother or a son killed by the Germans.

They gazed with hatred in the direction from which
the column was to appear. At last we saw it.

The Generals marched at the head, massive chins
stuck out, lips folded disdainfully, their whole
demeanour meant to show superiority over their
plebeian victors.

The women were clenching their fists. The soldiers
and policemen had all they could do to hold them back.

All at once something happened to them. They saw
German soldiers, thin, unshaven, wearing dirty,
bloodstained bandages, hobbling on crutches or leaning on the shoulders of their comrades; the soldiers
walked with their heads down.

The street became dead silent – the only sound was
the shuffling of boots and the thumping of crutches.

Then I saw an elderly woman in broken-down boots
push herself forward and touch a policeman's shoulder,
saying: 'Let me through.' There must have been some-

thing about her that made him step aside.

She went up to the column, took from inside her coat something wrapped in a coloured handkerchief and unfolded it. It was a crust of black bread. She pushed it awkwardly into the pocket of a soldier, so exhausted that he was tottering on his feet. And now suddenly from every side women were running towards the soldiers, pushing into their hands bread, cigarettes, whatever they had.

The soldiers were no longer enemies. They were people.

Yevtushenko

Comment   Seeing others that we dislike as people like us; with a Mum and Dad, brothers and sisters and friends, is a start to trying to understand and respect them.

Poster   *See* PT 22, 'Peace begins with a smile', *or* PT 29, 'The smile you send out returns to you'. *Poster may now be shown with the comment after reading the caption.*
Alternatively, Argus 42653-A, 'Speak kind words and you will hear kind echoes'.

Reading 2   Here are practical suggestions from Benjamin Franklin on respect for others:
The best thing to give your enemy is forgiveness.
— to an opponent, tolerance;
— to a friend, your ear;
— to your child, good example;
— to a father, reverence;
— to your mother, conduct that will make her proud of you;
— to yourself, respect;
— to all men, charity.

Closing record   'All you need is love', Beatles, Parlophone R 5620.

A8   Judging Others

Opening record *Introduce with description of what it is.*
Noye's Fludde, Benjamin Britten, 2NF1, *track* 'Mrs Noah's refusal'.

Comment   Could you make out the words of Mrs Noah's attitude? That's what we call 'prejudice'. But what is prejudice? Jimmy Savile calls it 'abuse of the mind'.

Reading 1   I dislike abuse of the mind. I was in Northern Ireland on one of my frequent trips to that place and there was a nice lady, and I said to her, 'How do you get on with the violence?' She says, 'It's awful, Jimmy, but the danger is that we're learning to live with it now. We've come to expect it and we just look at it and read about it and learn to live with it. It is a great sadness to us.' Then, she carried on in the same tone of voice, 'I will never be happy until every Catholic in Northern Ireland is dead.'

That saddened me beyond measure because there was the dear lady abusing her mind, unfortunately. It is an abuse of the mind to want to kill either Protestants or Catholics, or anybody or anything.

Jimmy Savile, *God'll Fix It*

Comment   Let us listen to what a few famous writers have to say about 'abuse of the mind' or prejudice.

READER A   'Prejudice is the child of ignorance.'

William Hazlitt

READER B   'To be prejudiced is always to be weak.'

Samuel Johnson

READER C   'Prejudices are what rule the vulgar crowd.'

Voltaire

READER D   'The man who never alters his opinion is like standing water, and breeds reptiles of the mind.'

William Blake

Comment   It is possible to change your opinion; to think deeply and rid your mind of any abuse that may fill it.

Reading 2   Air Commodore MacDonald Somerville saw a young punk rock group tramp out into a hazardous Scottish blizzard and succeed in rescuing a couple who almost certainly would otherwise have died.

'I always thought of pop groups as hairy kids pumping away on their ukeleles', he says, 'but these are very fine young fellows with a terrific social conscience.

'We've all got trenchant views, blinkered prejudices, and the tendency to slap labels on people. This might teach some of us to accept that punk rockers can be brave . . . teenagers can be responsible . . . missionaries can be bounders.'

Daily Mail

Comment   The air commodore came to realise that he had been quite wrong about a certain group of young people. We must all aim to have open and informed minds free from abuse.

Closing record   *Repeat opening track from Noye's Fludde.*

A9   **Personal Integrity**

There follow four very short role-plays. The four can take place in the same assembly area, pupils standing up to perform their piece and then sitting down again where they are.

Role-play 1   *A pupil is obviously waiting for someone – strolls up and down, looks at watch, etc. – another pupil appears and goes to walk by. First says,* 'Where have you been, I've been waiting half an hour.' 'Sorry,' *says the second,* 'I changed my mind, I'm going with Paul instead.' *He then walks on unconcerned.*

Comment   Integrity means you can be relied upon.

Role-play 2   *Two pupils wander into view – first says,* 'You can trust me, I'll not tell anyone, honest.' 'Well, all right,' *says the second. They whisper together for a moment. The second says,* 'See you later,' *and disappears. Another pupil appears and the first goes deliberately up to him – they whisper, then start laughing.*

Comment   Integrity means you can be trusted.

Role-play 3   *Child–Adult role play; one pupil should be taller and apparently older than the other.* 'Paul', *says the 'adult'.* 'I've told you before don't do that.' 'But, Dad', *says Paul*, 'you do it all the time.' 'That's got nothing to do with it,' *says Dad*, 'it doesn't matter what I do, you do what you are told.'

Comment   Integrity means there's a 'wholeness' or unity between what you say and what you do.

Role-play 4   *Child–Adult role play, as above.* 'I'm all ready, Dad, what time are we off?' 'Er, well we're not going,' *says Dad*. 'We're not going, why not?' *says son*. 'Well I forgot all about it, and now I'm too busy,' *replies the father*. 'But you promised,' *says son*. 'You've promised before and we didn't go.'

Comment   Integrity means you are a person of your word.

READER   This story shows that integrity can sometimes demand bravery, to match words with deeds.

During the Second World War, the people of Giazza (*pronounced 'Jatza'*), a village north of Verona, decided not to co-operate with a unit of German paratroopers stationed in their village. The commanding officer retaliated. He arrested a group of villagers and threatened to shoot them. The parish priest, Father Domenico Mercante, pleaded for his people and offered himself in their place. The Germans accepted his offer and prepared to execute him. One of the firing squad refused to shoot the priest. For his disobedience he was placed next to the priest and both died together. The soldier's name is not known.

Years passed and on the sixteenth anniversary of their deaths, on the spot where they died, a white monument to the two heroes was erected. Present at the ceremony was the Bishop of Verona, the German ambassador to Italy and the Italian Minister of Justice, who said, 'The example of a priest and soldier dying by the same rifle-fire, in order that not only the written law but the unwritten law too should be respected, provides an example of great moral value. It gives rise to the hope that the cause of peace amongst men may find its strongest protection in the conscience of humble but heroic spirits.'

Comment   'In the conscience of humble but heroic spirits.' That means ordinary people like you and me, being brave about standing up for real values.

A10   Respect for Property

Opening record 'Money, Money, Money', Abba, Epic EPC 4713

Comment   Do you remember *Oliver*, the musical based on Dickens's book *Oliver Twist*? In *Oliver*, Fagin had a school for pickpockets who went out to make money by picking the pockets of the rich. Gangs of boy pickpockets still 'work' in London today. Nowadays, they concentrate on the crowds of ordinary people and tourists in groups and on the London underground.

Role-play   *Pupil wheels an imaginary bike (a real bike could be used) into view, stands it up against a wall and goes into a shop. Another pupil comes along, looks around and gets on the bike, he's just about to ride off when the first pupil appears and says,* 'Oh, what are you doing, that's my bike.' 'Sorry', *says the second pupil,* 'I was only borrowing it for a ride.'

Comment   Taking without our permission is stealing (or shoplifting); 'borrowing' a classmate's biro and not returning it, could be stealing. There's a character in *Oliver* called, you'll remember, the Artful Dodger. If you are an artful dodger you could be a thief. To deliberately dodge paying your fare on the bus is to steal. You have taken a ride for nothing. Our attitude should be that we share and give rather than take. Jimmy Savile has this to say:

Reading   I try to use such monies as I have to do the sort of work of which I think God might be proud – sorting out a few human beings. But you have to be very, very careful about giving money away; you can actually ruin people. You have to be very sensitive about what you do with money. In principle, I don't mind having big lumps of money around me because I am forever doing things with the money. I don't exploit anyone to get hold of it; I still get it by luck and because I am pretty well known now.

Comment   Jimmy Savile is saying 'It's not what we have that's important, but the sort of people we are.'

(Show poster and read caption)

Poster   Argus 42081-A: 'It's not how much we have, but how much we enjoy that makes happiness.'

Christian Festivals

B11   Christmas I – Emmanuel

Opening record   Handel's *Messiah*, chorus, 'For unto us a child is born'.

Comment   That stirring opening chorus is from the *Messiah* by George Frederick Handel. Just before that piece, in the whole work, there are the words, 'The people who walked in darkness have seen a great light.' Handel himself knew what it was to be depressed and in the dark.

Reading   One night in 1741 a bent old man shuffled listlessly down a dark London street. George Frederick Handel was starting out on one of his aimless despondent wanderings. His mind was a battleground between hope and despair. For 40 years he had written stately music for the kings and queens of England, but now the court society had turned against him. Four years before, he had suffered a cerebral haemorrhage, which had paralysed his right side, making it impossible for him to walk or write. Slowly he had regained his strength and the ability to both walk and write. But now, aged 60, with England in the grip of a hard winter, he felt old and helplessly tired.

As he walked he passed a church, and welling up from within him came the cry, 'My God, my God, why have you forsaken me?' He returned to his shabby lodgings. On his desk was a bulky package. He opened it and his eye fell on the words, 'He was despised and rejected of men'. Reaching for a pen he started to write. Notes filled page after page. He worked almost non-stop for 24 days, taking little rest and even less food. When the *Messiah* lay finished on his desk he collapsed on his bed and slept for 17 hours. This tremendous masterpiece, one of the greatest ever composed, is now a traditional part of both Christmas and Easter.

Comment	Handel was not the first to imagine he was abandoned by God, only to find that God was with him all the time.
READER A	God asked Moses to go to the Egyptian Pharaoh and get his people released from slavery, but Moses was afraid. He said to God, 'Who am I to go to Pharaoh and bring the sons of Israel out of Egypt?' 'I shall be with you', God answered.

Exodus 3:12

Comment	God chose Joshua to take Moses' place as the leader of the Israelites, but he too was afraid.
READER B	God said to Joshua 'As long as you live, no one shall be able to stand in your way; I will be with you as I was with Moses; I will not leave you or desert you.'

Joshua 1:4

Comment	God asked Gideon to lead 300 men against an army of thousands from Midian. Gideon was terrified.
READER C	'My clan', said Gideon, 'is the weakest and I am the least important in my family.' God answered him, 'I will be with you and you shall crush Midian as though it were a single man.'

Judges 6:15

Comment	What happens when God sends his son to be the Light of the World?
READER D	The Lord himself, therefore, will give you a sign. It is this: 'The maiden is with child and will soon give birth to a son whom she will call Emmanuel.'

Isaiah 7:14–15

Comment	Emmanuel means 'God-is-with-us'.
Poster	*A poster may profitably be displayed at this point; without a caption. See* Argus Poster Gallery 33011-A *and* 33012-A, *or* 47027-A *for use with a small group.*
Record	*(Turned up to fade in on above)* Messiah, *chorus, 'For unto us a child is born'.*
Prayer	Almighty Father, you sent your son Jesus to be the Light of the World, the God-with-us. When all seems

dark around and depressing help us to remember that you are with us, always with us, whether we are enjoying good times or bad.

B12 Christmas II – Christ's Birthday

Comment   Did you know that the very first Christmas card was sent in 1844, by a Mr Dobson? The first cards to be sold publicly in the shops didn't come for another two years in 1846. The first company to produce large numbers of cards for sale was Tucks – who still make and sell cards – in the year 1870. It's hard to imagine Christmas now without cards, rather like birthdays without birthday cards.

Is it anyone's birthday today? Or tomorrow? Let's now sing 'Happy Birthday'.

Song   'Happy Birthday'.

Comment   Why don't we sing 'Happy Birthday' on Christmas Day, for Jesus Christ, instead of carols? It *is* his birthday, after all.

Reading 1   The first Christmas that little Linda learned to read she was allowed to distribute the family gifts on Christmas morning. According to family custom the one who distributed the gifts could open the first package. After all the presents were distributed with loving care, Linda kept looking and looking around the tree and among its branches. Finally her father asked, 'What are you looking for, dear?' To which Linda replied, 'I thought Christmas was Jesus' birthday and I was just wondering where his present is. I guess everyone forgot him.'

Anon.

Comment   I wouldn't be surprised if many of you could not tell me when your parents' birthdays are. Those who could tell me the date, I'm sure would not know the time of day their mother or father was born. If the day is so important why don't we know more about it? Another thought for you. Have you noticed that we usually only keep the birthdays of living people? So it's not the *day* that matters, but the person.

Reading 2   Birthdays are not about 'days' but about 'persons'. When my father's birthday comes round and I give him a card and a gift, I'm not really interested in what day of the year it is, I'm interested in him. My present says, 'I love you and I'm glad you're around.' I'm celebrating and being thankful for my father's continuing existence and all he's done for me.

Anon.

Comment   So at Christmas we are saying 'thank you' to Jesus for being still with us. On his birthday we celebrate that he is alive and among us still.

Prayer   On Christ's birthday, Almighty Father, we think too much of ourselves. Our thoughts centre upon presents, cards, trees, parties and food; we give little thought to your Son and his birthday. This Christmas help us not to be so selfish, help us to remember what we are celebrating. We are grateful and happy to have your Son alive and among us, may his birthday remind us of this. We offer our prayer through the same Christ our Lord. Amen.

(A suitable carol might be used to close the assembly)

B13   Christmas III – The Dignity of the Individual

Opening record 'Mary's boy child', Boney M, Atlantic K 11221 *(fade)*

Role-play   *There follows a short play which can be a straight part-reading or can be played out to the full.*

MARY   Now praise the Lord that led us
So safe into the town,
Where men will feed and bed us,
And I can lay me down.

JOSEPH	And how then shall we praise him? Alas my soul is sore That we no gifts can raise him, We are so very poor.
MARY	We have as much as any That on the earth do live, Although we have no penny, We have ourselves to give.
JOSEPH	Look yonder, wife, look yonder! A hostelry I see, Where travellers that wander Will very welcome be.
MARY	The house is tall and stately The door stands open thus; Yet, husband, I fear greatly That inn is not for us.
JOSEPH	God save you, gentle master! Your littlest room indeed With plainest walls of plaster Tonight will serve our need.
HOST	For lordlings and for ladies I've lodging and to spare; For you and yonder maid is No closet anywhere.
JOSEPH	Take heart, take heart, sweet Mary, Another inn I spy, Whose host will not be chary To let us easy lie.
MARY	O aid me, I am ailing, My strength is nearly gone; I feel my limbs are failing, And yet we must go on.
JOSEPH	God save you, hostess, kindly, I pray you, house my wife, Who bears beside me blindly The burden of her life.

HOSTESS	My guests are rich men's daughters And sons, I'd have you know! Seek out the poorer quarters Where ragged people go.
JOSEPH	Good sir, my wife's in labour, Some corner, let us keep.
HOST	Not I; knock up my neighbour, And as for me, I'll sleep.
JOSEPH	Good woman, I implore you, Afford my wife a bed.
HOSTESS	Nay, nay, I've nothing for you, Except the cattle shed.
MARY	Then gladly in the manger Our bodies we will house, Since men tonight are stranger Than asses are and cows.
JOSEPH	Take heart, take heart, sweet Mary, The cattle are our friends, Lie down, lie down, sweet Mary For here our journey ends.
MARY	Now praise the Lord that found me This shelter in the town, Where I with friends around me May lay my burden down.

Anon.

Comment   Have you ever noticed that Jesus started life in some-one's else's cattle shed and died 30 years later and was buried in someone else's tomb. Mary and Joseph had to 'seek out the poorer quarters where ragged people go'. They were poor but the most important people in the world at that moment. It's not what you have in life that matters — it's what sort of person you are. What matters is your dignity as an individual.

Litany Prayer

READER   When I say 'Lord, in your birth', please answer, 'we find our worth'.

In Bethlehem the first Christmas the people of Bethlehem put the rich before the poor. May we learn that
all men are equal, for Lord, in your birth

ALL   We find our worth.

READER   In Christ's life there were few possessions. May we
learn to put acquiring virtues before acquiring things,
for Lord, in your birth

ALL   We find our worth.

READER   In the quiet of the stable the Prince of Peace was born,
and in the fields the angels sang 'Goodwill to all men'.
May we be people of inner peace seeking to spread the
peace of Christ, for Lord, in your birth

ALL   We find our worth.

READER   In our celebration of Christmas we so easily forget that
our dignity as persons springs from the Word of God
becoming one of us. Help us Lord to realise our dignity
and worth, for Lord, in your birth

ALL   We find our worth.

*(The assembly could close with a suitable carol or a replay
of the opening record)*

B14   Easter I – Christ's Sacrifice and Death

Opening record   Handel's *Messiah*, part two, chorus 'All we like sheep
have gone astray' *(fade after 1 min. 40 sec.)*.

Comment   That magnificent chorus from Handel's *Messiah*
reminds us that the whole human race had strayed away
from God, rather like sheep without a shepherd to care
for them, so Christ came to die on the cross for us; to
make up to God for our selfishness.

*(For acting out the following story two pieces of wood, one
longer than the other, and both joined together in the shape*

of a cross, with a screw or nail, so that the cross piece is moveable. Four pupils required to wander on and pick up the wood in turn, and use it as directed.)

READER

Once upon a time there were two pieces of wood, fastened together by a nail or screw, and they lay on the sands, where, every day, when it was fine, children used to come and play.

Twice every day the tide came in and carried these pieces of wood backwards and forwards, leaving them on a different part of the beach each time. But when the tide had gone out the two pieces of wood were always there waiting for the children when they came onto the sands.

Lee came down early one morning, and he picked up the two pieces of wood which were very wet because the tide had only just gone out and he began to rush around the beach playing at aeroplanes. *(Pupil uses the cross as an aeroplane.)* But after about ten minutes he soon became tired and when he saw one of his friends coming down, he threw the two pieces of wood away and ran to meet him.

The next person to find the two pieces of wood was a little boy of seven called Peter. He came down to the sands after his tea and he had just been watching his favourite TV programme *Captain Pugwash*, all about pirates. So when he saw the pieces of wood he picked them up and began prancing around as though he were a pirate attacking a Spanish ship. *(Pupil brandishes the cross as a sword.)* But the sea was creeping in and over on the road Peter could see his father looking for him, so he soon forgot about the Spanish ship and left the wood to be carried backwards and forwards once more by the tide.

The next day was a Saturday, and that afternoon the beach was very crowded with people who had come down to the beach for the day. Among these were Mr and Mrs Simpson and their son Paul aged ten, and it was not long before Paul stumbled over something and picked it up. 'Look, I've got a machine gun', he shouted. 'A–a–a–a–a–a–a–a–a' *(pupil holds cross-bar vertical, putting it up to his eye and using it as a gun).*

After tea, Susan came down to the sands with her dog Sandy, she liked to come down as often as she could so that she could throw pieces of old driftwood into the sea, because Sandy liked nothing better than to run into the water and carry them back to Susan. She looked this way and that along the beach for a suitable piece of wood, and at last her eyes rested on the wood which Paul had been playing with a short time ago. 'This will do', she thought. She went across and pulled it out of the sand and straightened the cross-piece — and held it up like this +. 'Why, this is a cross', she said, 'a cross made out of rough wood — a miniature of the kind of cross on which Jesus died. I wonder why no one has seen it before. What a shame for it to be lying here, I know what I'll do, our Sunday School is having an Easter Garden next week in Church. I'll take this cross along and see if we can use it in the Garden'.

D.A. Willoughby

Comment There is a beautiful Anglo-Saxon poem, probably written about the year AD 750, over 1,200 years ago, which also views Christ's death for us on Calvary from the point of view of the cross itself. Here are some extracts from it.

READER A Listen to me.
I want to tell you the best dream I ever had,
It happened in the middle of the night,
When all men everywhere were sleeping in their beds.
It was just as if I saw a wonderful tree
Towering up into the sky.
It seemed to be filled with light,
Brighter than any light you've ever seen:
The whole gleaming shape was covered with gold.
And then I heard it begin to make a sound:
The wood itself, the best wood that could be found,
Began to talk to me like this:

READER B It was a long time ago . . .
But I can still remember it.
I was at the edge of the forest:
The last tree in the row.

They cut me down:
Left my roots behind.

Strong enemies there took me away:
They told me to hold their criminals up high:
They made me into an exhibition.

Men carried me on their shoulders,
Set me up on a hill.
And there a crowd of enemies
Fastened me firm in the ground.

Then I saw the Lord of all mankind
Hurry towards me eagerly,
He was determined to climb up on me.

He was intent on saving man,
The world over,
And I trembled as he
Laid himself upon me
In a kind of embrace.

But I still dared not bend down to the earth,
Or fall to the ground.
I had to stand up straight.
I was a Cross
I held up high
The King himself: the Lord of Power.
The Lord of Heaven above:
How could I stoop down?

They pierced me with dark nails:
You can still see the scars quite clearly:
Open wounds, inflicted by men of hate,
But I was powerless to harm them.

The crowd mocked us both:
I felt the moisture of the blood
From the man's side,
And then he let his spirit flee,
And died.

There were many grim experiences for me
On that hill.

from *Many Lights*, ed. D.G. Butler

Poster	*Poster* PT 78 *or* PT 111 *might be used at this point for a small group.*
Song	'Were you there when they crucified my Lord?' (CH 347, FH I 99, FP 40, HON 296, PL 190) *sung by a soloist, group or the whole assembly – or repeat the opening record.*

B15   Easter II – Risen Lord

Opening Comment	An important part of our business in this school is to impart and acquire knowledge. But there are different kinds of knowledge, or we can 'know' in different ways. For example:
READER A	I know French, I speak with a good French accent.
READER B	I know my way through London, I've often been by car.
READER C	I know how to crochet, I've made a lovely shawl.
READER D	I know Ron Greenwood, I can get Cup Final tickets.
READER E	I know Christ is alive and living among us.
Record	Handel's *Messiah*, part three, air, 'I know that my Redeemer liveth' *(fade after 2 min.).*
Comment	Thomas the Apostle came to know Jesus was alive. He would not believe when he was told by the other friends of Jesus. He had to learn the truth of it for himself.
Dramatic Reading	*Reading for Narrator/Jesus/Thomas and small group: scene — the upper room in Jerusalem.*
NARRATOR	The first day of the week passed and it was now late in the evening. The friends of Jesus were together in the house. They had locked the doors because they were frightened of the Jewish leaders. Then — there was Jesus standing among them.
JESUS	Peace be with you.

NARRATOR	With these words, he let them see his hands and his side. They saw it was Jesus and were overjoyed.
JESUS	Peace be with you. The Father sent me on a mission now I am sending you.
NARRATOR	He there and then gave them God's power.
JESUS	Receive the Holy Spirit.
NARRATOR	That evening one of the friends of Jesus was absent — Thomas, nicknamed 'the twin'.
GROUP	(*speaking together*) We've seen the Lord.
NARRATOR	The others told him when he came back.
THOMAS	I don't believe it. I must see the nail-marks in his hands and touch them first and I must put my hand in his side. Then I'll believe.
NARRATOR	The following Sunday, the friends of Jesus were again in the house with locked doors. This time Thomas was there too. Suddenly Jesus was there with them again.
JESUS	Peace be with you.
NARRATOR	Then he turned to Thomas.
JESUS	Where are your fingers? Here are my hands. Touch my side with your hand. You must show that you trust, that you believe in me.
THOMAS	My Lord and my God.
JESUS	Do you believe in me and trust me just because you have seen me with your own eyes? Happy are the people who will trust me without ever having seen me with their own eyes.

Alan Dale, based on John 20:19–29

Prayer

READER	Happy are we if we can say 'I know my redeemer lives'. Please join in this response: 'Lord, we know you are alive and to be found among us.' I am risen and can be found among you.

ALL	Lord, we know you are alive and can be found among us.
READER	I am risen and you can hear my words in the words of the Bible.
ALL	Lord, we know, *etc.*
READER	I am risen and can be found in service to your neighbour.
ALL	Lord, we know, *etc.*
READER	I am risen and among you when you are gathered together in my name.
ALL	Lord, we know, *etc.*
READER	I am risen and you can find me in the breaking of bread.
ALL	Lord, we know, etc.
Closing record	Handel's *Messiah*, part two, chorus 'Hallelujah', *fade in* 'King of Kings' *etc.*

B16   Easter III – Living Lord

Opening Song/ Record	'Morning has broken' (CH 196, FH I 73, FP 196, HON 171, NL 79, SLW 9) *may be sung, or play the record:* Cat Stevens, Island WIP 6121.
Comment	*(If size of group permits, poster PT 3 may be shown here)*
	On the very first morning of creation, the world was probably a fiery ball of gas. With the resurrection from the dead of Jesus, the Son of God, we have a new creation: 'Morning has broken like the first morning.'
Role-play	*Four pupils enter, one carrying an Easter candle (the local parish church might be kind enough to lend theirs for the occasion). The candle has been prepared with long white paper streamers about an inch wide, attached to the top of the candle. The candle is held aloft and the other pupils,*

taking hold of the streamers, walk slowly round the candle. The streamers wind round the candle, maypole fashion. Meanwhile a comment is made.

Comment   On the streamers are your names, written (*yesterday/ this morning or whenever*) in your own handwriting. At your christening you were given a candle as a symbol of your oneness with Christ, the light of the World. The streamers have become one with the candle — you are one with Christ the Light of the World. (*The candle is placed in a central position.*)

Reading 1   One ancient symbol of Christian belief in the resurrection is the phoenix. This bird symbolised hope and the continuity of life after death.

According to legend, only one phoenix could live at a time. The Greek poet Hesiod, writing in the eighth century BC, said it lived nine times the lifespan of the long-living raven. When the bird felt death approaching, it built itself a pyre of wild cinnamon and died in the flames. But from the ashes there then arose a new phoenix, which tenderly encased its parent's remains in an egg of myrrh and flew with them to the Egyptian city of Heliopolis, where it laid them on the Altar of the Sun. These ashes were said to have the power of bringing a dead man back to life.

Scholars now think that the germ of the legend came from the Orient, and was adopted by the sun-worshipping priests of Heliopolis as an allegory of the sun's daily setting and rebirth.

In Christian art the resurrected phoenix became a popular symbol of Christ risen from the grave.

Comment   The phoenix is an ancient symbol of the resurrection of Christ. The writer D.H. Lawrence has a poem that applies the symbol to our lives.

Reading 2   *Phoenix*
Are you willing to be sponged out, erased, cancelled, made nothing?
Are you willing to be made nothing?
Dipped into oblivion?

If not, you will never really change.

The phoenix renews her youth
only when she is burnt, burnt alive, burnt down
to hot and flocculent ash.
Then the small stirring of a new small bub in the
nest with strands of down like floating ash,
Shows that she is renewing her youth like the eagle,
Immortal bird.

D.H. Lawrence

Comment   Our baptism candle was given to us with the words
'keep this flame burning brightly'. We can only do that
if we try to stay close to Christ, the Light of the World.

Song   'Now the green blade riseth' (CH 53, FH II 14, HON 181,
NL 36, PL 201).

B17   Pentecost I – Symbol of Fire

Comment   If I was to shout out now, 'Fire, Fire,' and the fire
alarm sounded, you would probably think, 'it's not a
fire drill this time, or a false alarm, but the real thing.'
Some of you might be frightened. Fire can be frighten-
ing – think of the fear of people trapped by fire in a
hotel or big store, or the film, *Towering Inferno*.

READER A   Fire can destroy – I often help my dad burn the dried
weeds and leaves in the garden.

READER B   Fire can be welcoming – we have a coal fire at home and
when I come in wet and cold from snowballing or
football in the winter, it's great to sit by the fire.

READER C   Fire is strong – I went on an outing once to an iron
foundry where we saw great cauldrons of melted iron,
taken out of the massive furnaces.

READER D   Fire can give light – I remember when there was an
electricity strike and we only had candles alight in the
house. I was surprised how much light one candle
gives.

Comment   Fire has been important to man over the centuries – for cooking as well as light; for warmth and life too. Listen to this extract from a story by Jack London, about a man travelling in the Arctic in weather 75 degrees below freezing point. He is travelling alone in snow-covered country and has just fallen and got his feet wet.

READER A

He would have to build a fire and dry out his footgear. This was imperative at that low temperature – he knew that much; and he turned aside to the bank, which he climbed. On top, tangled in the underbush about the trunks of several small spruce trees, was a highwater deposit of dry firewood – sticks, and twigs, principally, but also larger portions of seasoned branches and fine, dry last year's grasses. He threw down several large pieces on top of the snow. This served for a foundation and prevented the young flame from drowning itself in the snow it otherwise would melt. The flame he got by touching a match to a small shred of birch bark that he took from his pocket. This burned even more readily than paper. Placing it on the foundation, he fed the young flame with wisps of dry grass and with the tiniest dry twigs.

He worked slowly and carefully, keenly aware of his danger. Gradually, as the flame grew stronger, he increased the size of the twigs with which he fed it. He squatted in the snow pulling the twigs out from their entanglement in the brush and feeding directly to the flame. He knew there must be no failure. When it is seventy-five below zero, a man must not fail in his attempt to build a fire – that is, if his feet are wet.

But he was safe. Toes and nose and cheeks would be only touched by the frost, for the fire was beginning to burn with strength. He was feeding it with twigs the size of his finger. In another minute he would be able to feed it with branches the size of his wrist, and then he could remove his wet footgear and, while it dried, he could keep his naked feet warm by the fire, rubbing them at first, of course, with snow. The fire was a success. He was safe.

Comment

But he wasn't; a moment later a branch-load of snow cascaded on the fire and buried it. After he had recovered from his bitter disappointment he desperately swung his arms to and fro to try to get warm, then tried again. But his fingers were now frost-bitten and he had to light the bark holding the matches in the palm of his hand.

READER B   At last, when he could endure no more, he jerked his hands apart. The blazing matches fell sizzling into the snow, but the birch bark was alight. He began laying dry grasses and the tiniest twigs on the flame. He could not pick and choose, for he had to lift the fuel between the heels of his hands. Small pieces of rotten wood and green moss clung to the twigs, and he bit them off as well as he could with his teeth. He cherished the flame carefully and awkwardly. It meant life, and it must not perish. The withdrawal of blood from the surface of his body now made him begin to shiver and he grew more awkward. A large piece of green moss fell squarely on the little fire. He tried to poke it out with his fingers, but his shivering frame made him poke too far, and he disrupted the nucleus of the little fire, the burning grasses and tiny twigs separating and scattering. He tried to poke them together again, but in spite of the tenseness of the effort, his shivering got away with him, and the twigs were hopelessly scattered. Each twig gushed a puff of smoke and went out.

Comment   That was his last living effort — shortly afterwards he died of the bitter cold.

Comment   The Spirit of God has been symbolised throughout the Bible, as a fire; a fire that warms, a fire that lights up, a fire that burns rubbish away.

Scripture reading   Acts 2:1–3.

Prayer   Come Holy Spirit, give life to our souls, light up our minds with your fire; destroy our selfishness and warm our hearts with the fire of your love. Make us clean within, by your purifying fire, so that we may better serve the Son of God and give greater glory to the Father. Amen.

Song   'Holy Spirit of fire' (CH 125, FH II 7, FP 90) *or* 'Holy Spirit, Lord of light' (CH 124, HON 109, PL 216).

B18   Pentecost II – Symbol of Wind

Comment   Newspaper headlines: 'How I survived the waves of death'. In 1979 the famous yacht race, from Cowes on the Isle of Wight to Ireland and back – round the Fastnet Rock – ran into the most terrible storm ever experienced in that area. Many boats were lost, 138 people were rescued, and 17 sailors lost their lives. This is one man's story in a local evening paper.

READER   A Southend yachtsman has spoken of the most terrifying experience of his life – the storm-hit Fastnet Race. Richard Hughes, 29, of Westcliff, relived the nightmare of the disastrous race that claimed the lives of 17 sailors.

He was one of the nine-man crew on the 37 foot yacht *Zap* – a sister ship to the Burnham boat *Trophy*, which lost three men.

Richard is an experienced yachtsman but it was his first Fastnet.

He has sailed in a transatlantic race and endured a hurricane in the Bermuda Cup ocean race.

He said: 'I have sailed through a hurricane, but it was nothing like this. This storm was so severe for so long. The waves were mountainous – the height of a double-decker bus. Great high walls were topped with rolling crests that smashed against the boat. At first we had too much sail up. We were racing so fast the speedo was off the clock.'

Richard said luck and applied seamanship saved his yacht from catastrophe.

Safety harnesses stopped him being washed overboard as he struggled along the deck.

As he looked back, a wave engulfed the yacht and he saw his helmsman up to his chest in water.

'It was terrifying. The waves were smashing over us and the boat was gyrating about at all angles. Crew

morale was low. We were about two-thirds of the way
to Ireland when the storm stuck', said Richard.

Zap wandered up and down the Irish coast for a day
and night before getting into Cork harbour.

Basildon Evening Echo

Comment Mountainous seas in a storm are caused by the wind,
which whips up the waves. The wind is a very powerful
force.

READER A It can drive windmills. The wind can be harnessed for
good, to pump water and grind grain.

READER B It can dry washing on the clothes line and be a cooling
breeze on a very hot day.

READER C The wind can be gentle — and fun when I fly my kite!

READER D The wind is an invisible power which blows where it
will!

Comment The Holy Spirit is an invisible power that moves where
it will!

Reading Acts 2:1–4.

Reading (*This may be sung as a hymn: see* CH 357)
Where does the wind come from?
Where is it going?
You see the swaying tree,
and all the grasses blowing.
You know the wind is there,
but where?
There is no knowing.

Where does the Spirit come?
Where is his dwelling?
You see the weary world
so wilful, so rebelling.
But still the Spirit breathes
and where
there is no telling.

Sister Mary Oswin

Prayer Come Holy Spirit, breath of God, blow away the cob-
webs of selfishness within us and guide us to a close

union with Jesus, to the glory of God the Father. Amen.

B19   Pentecost III – Symbol of Breath

Comment
Without air your football or your bike tyres aren't much use. A football lacks form, 'life' – if you like – without air; your bike becomes 'dead' it there's no air in the tyres.

Role-play
The scene is a busy beach in the middle of the summer holidays. A group of teenagers see a boy in trouble out in the sea (group drifts on to the stage or area, talking together). One of the group cries out, 'Look, someone's drowning, come on, Tony.' *Two boys disappear. Others stand looking anxiously, then one comments,* 'They've got him – here they come.' *Another says,* 'Come on, let's help.' *A boy is hauled into view, unconscious. One of the rescuers says,* 'What shall we do now?' 'I'll go for an ambulance' *says a girl.* 'I'll call the police', *says another.* 'No, no', *says a third,* 'That will all be too late. He needs the kiss of life. I've learnt it at Scouts. Quick, out of the way.' *He kneels down by the boy and gives the kiss of life. Unconscious boy recovers slowly. Sits up. Girl who rushed off to get ambulance comes back calling,* 'The ambulance is here.'

Comment
It is a wonderful thing to know how to breathe life back into someone – to give them life again. God first breathed life into us.

Scripture reading
Genesis 2:5–7.

Comment
The Holy Spirit breathes new life into Christians so that they may live more fully for God and those around them.

Reading
The Holy Spirit
As glass is soft
And molten in the flame

And moulded by the craftsman's loving hand;
As trees can bow and dance
Before the wind
To music piped from where the rushes stand;
As breath gives life
And power to the arm
To pull the oar and raise the haycock high;
The dove of peace
Is shielding us from harm
He hovers in the hearts of you and I.

His fire can warm
And mould me tall and strong.
His wind blows through
My prayer, praise and song.
His Breath fills me with life
So I can be
A sign of love and peace
For all to see.

Christy Kenneally

Hymn 'Breathe on me, breath of God' (AM 236, CH 37, HON 34, NL 86, PL6).

B20 The Holy Trinity

Comment The most terrible punishment that can be inflicted upon a person is to be cut off from every other human for a long period; it is called solitary confinement. It is such a terrible experience because we are each made to love and be loved – we are made to be with others.

READER A An ITN reporter interviewed a missionary working in Malaysia with the 'Boat People' – the thousands of refugees driven out of Vietnam and escaping in old battered boats. Only half of the tens of thousands ever arrived in a new country – the rest were lost at sea in storms, or drowned when sinking boats went down or attacked and killed by pirates. The ITV newsman said to the missionary, 'Does the depressing sight of these poor people make you doubt the existence of God?' 'No', replied the missionary, 'it convinces me that there must be something better than man. There must be a power of love beyond man.'

READER B   St Augustine was a great Christian thinker and writer who lived about AD 400. One day he was walking along the sea-shore thinking about the mystery of the Trinity and how he could best describe it in a book he was writing. Close by he saw a little boy, who had dug a hole in the sand and was running to and fro to the sea with his bucket, pouring water into the hole. 'What are you trying to do?' asked Augustine. 'I am going to put all the sea into that hole', replied the little boy. Yes, thought Augustine to himself, that is like me, trying to put into human words the vast mystery of God.

He went home and wrote his book about the Trinity, in which he says that God is love, therefore, there must be somehow more than one in God; that the Father and Son love each other and the Love which proceeds from them is the Holy Spirit. That is the nearest we can get to so deep a mystery.

Prayer

READER   To every third invocation, please reply, 'Praise and glory to your name.'

Father, creator of our vast universe,
Father, creator of our daily world,
Father, giver of life and love,

ALL   Praise and glory to your name.

READER   Son of God, saviour of all,
Son of God, sharer of our daily world,
Son of God, giver of life and love,

ALL   Praise and glory to your name.

READER   Holy Spirit, inspirer of truth and love,
Holy Spirit, comforter in out daily world,
Holy Spirit, giver of life and love,

ALL   Praise and glory to your name.

Christian Calling and Life

C21   Christian Vocation

Opening record *Background* Stravinsky's *Rite of Spring, track*, 'The Sacrifice', ASD 2315 (*fade*).

Comment Today we start a serial – a story told in five parts over the next five assemblies. The story is by Nigel Sustins and is called 'Climb the Dark Wall'.

READER They sat cross-legged on the ground in a circle. Tim was the one with the sandy hair and wandering eyes, Maureen with the swinging black pony-tail, Douglas pale and thin-faced, Jenny with cheeks the colour of sun-ripened apples and Philip was the tallest of them. They were trying to hold down a fit of the giggles as the teacher droned on, turning over oily pieces of machinery that were meant to fit into a sensible shape. Machines! That was all they were ever taught about. 'Tomorrow', said the teacher, without taking his dull unblinking eyes off the metal pieces, 'you will visit the factory where you will work as soon as you are old enough.'

'What excitement,' they thought!

The next day a ramshackle old truck groaned into their commune and they crouched down in the back, ready to discover the delights that lay ahead in their adult life when they would be able to work for the state.

At midday the truck rattled to a halt and the 'teachers' (they were really black-uniformed state guards) made the children get out and sit at the roadside to eat a quick lunch. A cloud seemed to pass over the sun as they chewed their rations and the guards started to nod off in to sleep.

'That's odd!' said Tim. 'These fellows must work harder than we thought!' There was a crunch of boots on the roadway and the children looked up to see the remarkable face of a stranger. He was bearded and sun-tanned, with travel-stained outdoor clothes, a rucksack on his back and a coil of rope over one shoulder. His eyes gleamed good-humouredly.

'They sleep soundly, the mindless ones! Come! We'll have a different lesson today. I've something more interesting than factories to show you.'

'But . . . who are you?' asked Philip. 'Where have you come from?'

'The hills. I'm a mountaineer. Call me Eagle. I sometimes get as high as that bird even without wings.'

He was walking away from them, and they all looked at each other, shrugged their shoulders and followed.

Comment	The important word in that story, which sums it all up, is 'Come'. The stranger calls Tim, Maureen, Douglas, Jenny and Philip to follow him.
Scripture reading	Matthew 4:18–22: 'As Jesus walked along the shore of Lake . . .' (*The* Good News Bible *is recommended for this and other Scripture readings.*)
Comment	Jesus called quite a number of people to follow him, to be his disciples, but not all answered the call.
Scripture reading	Matthew 19:16–22.
Prayer	Almighty Father, your Son calls us to follow him, to live the Christian life. It is not easy to live up to what he asks of us, so please give us the strength we need to answer his call courageously and generously. Amen.
Closing record	*Replay or bring up opening record.*

C22   Baptism

Opening record	Stravinsky's *Rite of Spring*, *track* 'Dance of young maidens', ASD 2315 *(fade).*
Comment	Today we continue our serial 'Climb the Dark Wall'.

Last time you will remember, Tim, Maureen, Douglas, Philip and Jenny are called away from a boring monotonous life by Eagle, the strange traveller.

Reading   Eagle stopped at the edge of a swift stream. 'First lesson', he said, uncoiling his rope and linking them all together with a loop round each waist. 'Let the rope be your lifeline. Feel it between your fingers and trust it.'

Eagle plunged straight into the stream.

'Hey!' shouted Maureen. 'Hang on! I've had a bath this week already!'

'Don't be timid. Come on. Trust the rope.'

One after another they waded into the rapid current until they were up to their chins in water. They could just see Eagle climbing up the bank on the other side in front of them. They had to go right under, mouths shut tight, and feel the pull of the rope drawing them through the stream.

They all dripped on the grass together, looking very sorry for themselves.

'Don't worry', said Eagle. 'We'll dry out. Second lesson: a little rock-climbing.'

They'd never had such a stiff climb in all their lives before, but Eagle shouted out instructions – where to place hands and feet and how to balance the body – and they managed to haul themselves to the summit of a grey-stone crag that overhung the valley.

'There!' said Eagle, pointing downwards. 'Smoke, factory walls. Chimneys like sooty fingers poking at the sky. They call it progress! Why do they love their walls so much?'

'S'pose they want to keep all the people in,' said Jenny. 'Otherwise, we'd all be off: no stopping in those rat-holes.'

'They also want to hide something,' said Eagle. 'Look: we can catch a glimpse of it from up here.'

He pointed into the distance where the puffy clouds over the mountain-tops thinned, and the children saw brief gleams like sunshine on smooth lakes or glinting from green-gold forests.

'Beautiful!' said Douglas. 'Where is it?'

'My land. I want to take you there. But first you have

to learn to climb. Because before we can get to my land, we have to scale the daddy of all black walls. It's built like a battleship and twice as thick.'

Comment 'Trust the rope', said Eagle, as they all plunged one at a time through the water. We became Christians when we were baptised. Then we started a new life of faith and trust in God – the rope in the story.

READER After each sentence please answer, 'No one can enter the Kingdom of God unless he is born through water and the Spirit.'

Jesus said, 'Lay not up for yourselves treasure upon earth, but lay up for yourselves treasure in heaven.'

ALL No one can enter the Kingdom of God unless he is born through water and the Spirit.

READER Jesus said, 'Unless you become like little children you shall not enter the Kingdom of God.'

ALL No one, *etc.*

READER Jesus said, 'What you do for the least person you do for me.'

ALL No one, *etc.*

READER Jesus said, 'Love your enemies, do good to those who dislike you.'

ALL No one, *etc.*

READER Jesus said, 'Ask and you shall receive, seek and you shall find, knock and the door will be opened to you.'

ALL No one, *etc.*

Poster *While the above is being said, the poster* Argus 42761-A *can be shown* – 'Where you come from is not nearly as important as where you are going'. *Alternatively, poster* PT 11 *may be used.*

Hymn 'The Lord's my Shepherd' (CH 312, HON 267, NL 92, PL 115, SLW 102) – *or replay the opening record.*

C23   Eucharist

Opening record   *Background* Stravinsky's *The Rite of Spring*, *track* 'Mystical circle of the young maidens', ASD 2315 (*fade*).

Comment   We continue now our serial story 'Climb the Dark Wall'. Maureen, Tim, Douglas, Philip and Jenny have gone with 'Eagle' away from the dark city to live in the mountains.

READER   It was a wonderful time – living in the hills with Eagle, and feeding on the coarse brown bread he produced and the refreshing drink that glowed in their veins like wine. But – too soon as far as they were concerned – he spoke to them one day with tight lips and a grim face. 'We've got to go down. Face the black wall. There's no escaping it.'

They picked their way through gullies and over rockfalls and came down to a darkened valley where the weak light that managed to struggle through showed up the grains of dust and grit littering the air. The wall reared its head like a black, square-faced whale on the peak of a tidal wave. Blank. Forbidding. Definitely saying: 'No through way.'

'How do we get over that?' whispered Maureen.

'Courage. Skill. And trust in your rope.' said Eagle.

'Now I'm going to . . .' he stopped in mid-sentence and cocked his ear to listen. 'A jeep!' he hissed. 'Patrol! Quick – up that bank and into the bushes, and keep the rope in your hands.'

'What are you going to do?' asked Philip.

'Climb the dark wall. It's beaten men for too long.'

'But the danger . . .'

'The danger is to be content with that ugly monster blocking out our joys and hopes. Someone has to climb the wall, or the fear of it will drag us all down to death.'

Comment   As part of their training with Eagle the children ate 'the coarse brown bread'. In our journey through life we may receive the bread to eat which is the body of Christ.

READER   After each sentence please answer 'Lord you are with us; may we find strength in the breaking of bread.'

Jesus said, 'Do not work for food that cannot last, but work for food the endures to eternal life.'

ALL   Lord, you are with us, *etc.*

READER   Jesus said, 'My father gives you bread from heaven, the true bread which gives life to the world.'

ALL   Lord, you are with us, *etc.*

READER   Jesus said, 'I am the bread of life. He who comes to me will never be hungry.'

ALL   Lord, you are with us, *etc.*

READER   Jesus said, 'If you do not eat the flesh of the Son of Man and drink his blood, you will not have life in you.'

ALL   Lord, you are with us, *etc.*

READER   Jesus said, 'He who eats my flesh and drinks my blood lives in me and I live in him.'

ALL   Lord, you are with us, *etc.*

Hymn   'Feed us now' (CH 72, FH I 103) *or* 'I am the bread of life' (CH 128, FH II 57, FP 144, HON 114). *Alternatively, play the opening music.*

C24   Faith

Opening record Stravinsky's *Rite of Spring*, *track* 'Sacrificial dance', ASD 2315 *(fade)*.

Comment   We left our story 'Climb the Dark Wall' with the group led by Eagle at the foot of the dark wall. They hear a jeep coming . . .

READER   The children hurried away into the bushes, and Eagle approached the wall. He rubbed his hands over the rough pitted surface and stared hard at it as if he could move it by force of will.

The sound of the patrol jeep grew louder. With painful slowness Eagle gripped the wall with fingers and toes and started to inch his way up the vertical climb. He breathed heavily but clung to the surface as if he were glued to it.

The jeep screeched to a standstill. A black figure rose up from the back seat and extended the silver nozzle of a high-velocity rifle. An ear-splitting whine, and Eagle was knocked off the wall as if he had been a fly.

Black-booted guards gathered round his body, kicked him and laughed. They dragged him towards the wall, and levered up a slab of stone which covered a gaping hole: a kind of tomb, airless and cold. Eagle's body was dumped inside the hole, and then the stone rammed home again. Sealed. Utter blackness.

The jeep grated its gears and drove off. The children looked out from the bushes with white sweating faces.

'Why?' asked Jenny, crying. 'What do we do now?'

'We wait,' said Tim. 'As he said. We've still got the rope.'

And all through the rest of that day and into the night that followed, they clung to the rope, feeling it to be indeed their only life-line.

Comment	'We've still got the rope' said Tim. They still had faith and hope – although all seemed desperate.
Scripture reading	Luke 23:44–49.

Prayer

READER	Let us pray for the lonely, the depressed and the bereaved. To each invocation please reply, 'Lord, help us to believe in you and trust you.' For those who are dying and who are afraid – give them strength and courage.
ALL	Lord, help us to believe in you and trust you.
READER	For those who have been wounded by the death of someone they love,
ALL	Lord, help us, *etc*.
READER	For those who are very ill and are in pain,
ALL	Lord, help us, *etc*.

READER	For those who are made unhappy by loneliness and depression,
ALL	Lord, help us, *etc.*
READER	When we are lonely, frightened and fed up,
ALL	Lord, help us, *etc.*
READER	When our parents, teachers and friends seem to misunderstand, and we feel like running away from it all,
ALL	Lord, help us, *etc.*
READER	When we find it hard to believe in your love and care,
ALL	Lord, help us, *etc.*
Song	'Give me joy in my heart' (CH 84, FH I 78, FP 105, HON 78, NL 63, NO 70, SLW 4) *or replay the opening music.*

C25   Mission

Opening record	Stravinsky's *Rite of Spring*, *track*, 'Dance of the adoration of earth', ASD 2315 *(fade)*.
Comment	Our story 'Climb the Dark Wall' finishes today. Last time Maureen, Tim and the others were left alone after the death of Eagle.
READER	It was still dark. But they sensed a change in the air. A humming. Enemy aircraft? No. A throbbing, like a huge sob or cheer about to break out. Then they heard the roar of an explosion. They tumbled head over heels out of the bushes and down the slope towards the black wall. Slowly they got to their feet. The rope: it was pulling, pulsing with life, tugging them up against the wall. They felt all over the black surface, and it seemed to them as if they were looking downward into the black ice of an enormous frozen lake. Then their hands broke through the ice, and they were wriggling their fingertips in air: an open space. A pin-prick of light sprang up as from a great distance, and started to spin round like a Catherine wheel, gaining in size and speed

as it spun down a black tunnel towards them. Suddenly: bright flame. Like the sun. Of course: the sun rising beyond the wall. They were seeing through the wall. No sooner had they realised that when a figure rose up in the tunnel – a human shape rimmed with fire. Eagle stepped out in front of them, the early sunlight flicking in his hair.

'Eagle!' they cried, breathless with wonder and excitement.

'What a climb!' he said, smiling at them. 'I have fallen to great depths, but see . . . I have climbed back again. The fear of death has left me unmarked.'

'But how? . . . We saw you shot . . . walled up . . .'

'Enough!' he said, raising his hand. 'This wall will never be impassable again. I have opened a way that can never be closed.'

'And can we go through?' asked Douglas. 'Into your land?'

'Not yet. You all have a job to do first of all. Bring more people to this place. Draw them from all parts of the world, from every nation and race. You have my rope and my promise of help. Join all humankind – yes, all the Universe – into the bonds of my rope which bring freedom.'

They stood looking at him amazed, tired, joyful, bewildered. He laughed and went from one to the other ruffling their hair.

'Go on, children. Go with my blessing.'

And they looked at each other, shrugged their shoulders and went.

Comment	'Go with my blessing', Eagle said. The group were sent out.
Scripture reading	Matthew 28:16–20.
Comment	If we really believe that Christ rose from the dead then we have an obligation to work and pray for more people to believe that too.
READER	Please respond to each invocation with the words, 'May your kingdom come.'

	Christ, our leader and friend, we pray that all people may come to know and love you.
ALL	May your kingdom come.
READER	That all men may work together to make the world a happier, more peaceful place to live in.
ALL	May your kingdom come.
READER	That the world's food and energy may be shared for the greatest good of all,
ALL	May your kingdom come.
READER	That the delicate balance of nature may not be destroyed by human greed or bad judgement,
ALL	May your kingdom come.
READER	That all the world's children may have the opportunities of education and good health,
ALL	May your kingdom come.
READER	That all people may learn to give dignity and respect to each and every one of their neighbours, whatever their race or religion.
ALL	May your kingdom come.
READER	Let us now say the prayer that Jesus taught us:
ALL	Our Father . . .
Song	'God's Spirit is in my heart' (CH 99, FH I 57, FP 35, HON 89, NL 116, SLW 93) *or replay the opening music*.

Old Testament

D26   Trust in God

Opening record 'Bright Eyes', Art Garfunkel, CBS 6947 (*introduction 1 min. 20 sec.*).

Comment   Once upon a time there was a wealthy Edomite sheik called Job, the most outstanding sheik in all the East. He was, moreover, a good man, a genuinely innocent man. His religion was real religion and he would have nothing to do with evil of any kind. He had a large family – seven sons and three daughters – and immense wealth.

Reading

NARRATOR   One day God summoned the Heavenly Court. It met in his presence and among the members of the court was 'The Satan', God's Inspector General.
      God turned to him.

GOD   Where have you been?

SATAN   On the earth. I've been wandering north, south, east and west.

GOD   Did you come across my servant Job? Now he's a good man for you – a genuinely innocent man. His religion is real religion and he won't have anything to do with evil of any kind.

SATAN   Yes, I met him. He's a good man, I admit. But then he has every reason to be! He has nothing to fear – you stand guard over him and his family and his wealth. Indeed, it is you who have made him as wealthy as he is. But just touch that wealth of his – or his family – and he'll curse you to your face!

GOD   Very well, he's in your hands – you do just that. But leave the man himself alone.

NARRATOR	Then Satan left the court (*pause*). One day the young people were having a banquet at the eldest son's house. Job himself was at home. Then disaster followed disaster. One after another messengers came running with news:
MESSENGER 1	Arab raiders have carried off the oxen and asses from the fields and murdered your herdsmen! I'm the only one to escape!
MESSENGER 2	Lightning has killed all your sheep and shepherds! I'm the only one to escape!
MESSENGER 3	Wild tribes from the desert – three bands of them – have driven your camels off and killed all your camel-drivers! I'm the only one to escape!
MESSENGER 4	A desert hurricane has blown your son's house down. The young people were buried in the rubble – and they're all dead! I'm the only one to escape!
NARRATOR	Job was hard hit. But he knelt down in prayer:
JOB	I came naked from the earth, to the earth I shall go naked back. God gave, God takes back – Blessed be his name!
NARRATOR	All through these disasters Job never lost his trust in God – or said a word against him. Things got even worse for Job. God allowed Satan to tempt him further. Satan went back to earth. He struck Job with boils from head to foot, and Job sat itching in the ash-pit scratching himself with a piece of broken crockery. His wife scolded him.
JOB'S WIFE	And you still trust him! Curse him – and die!
JOB	That's a wicked thing to say. You're talking just like a street gossip! You know that we must take God on his own terms, whether it's good or evil he sends. That's no more than our duty.

NARRATOR   Job is left with nothing – not even good health; but Satan does not shake his trust in God.

Play the record 'Bright Eyes' *(as above); fade to background for reading.*

God gave Job everything back – indeed he made him twice as wealthy as he had been before.

His kinsmen and friends held a banquet in his honour. They sat down together at table and consoled him for all the misfortunes he had gone through. They each gave him a silver coin and a gold ring.

Job's wealth was now immense. And he had a second family – seven sons and three daughters as before. The girls were the most beautiful girls in the world (he called the youngest 'Bright Eyes') and in his will he went beyond the law and treated them like their brothers.

He lived for a long time after this. He had great-great-grandchildren, and was a very old man when he died.

Alan T. Dale, *Winding Quest*

Prayer   *Psalm 139*
Lord, you examine me and know me,
you know if I am standing or sitting,
you read my thoughts from far away,
whether I walk or lie down, you are watching,
you know every detail of my conduct.

God examine me and know my heart,
probe me and know my thought;
make sure I do not follow evil ways,
and guide me in the way that is everlasting.

Hymn   'Lord of all hopefulness', CH 181, HON 162, NL 54, NO 39, PL 288, SLW 44.

D27   Reconciliation

Opening record 'We don't talk anymore', Cliff Richard, EMI 2975 *(fade after 1 min. 30 sec.)*.

Comment   'We're not speaking to one another' you hear people say when they've fallen out with someone. God never 'falls out' with us – we fall out with him. Like King Ahab who approves of a terrible crime by his wife.

Reading

NARRATOR   Naboth was a farmer. His vineyard had belonged to his family for many generations and lay next to the palace grounds in Jezreel City. King Ahab asked Naboth one day about it.

KING AHAB   I'm wanting a vegetable garden. Your vineyard is just what I want – it's next-door to my palace. Will you let me have it? I'll give you a better vineyard for it; or I'll pay you a fair price, just as you like.

NABOTH   No, the vineyard was my father's and my grandfather's. I should be an irreligious man if I sold my ancestral lands.

NARRATOR   The king went back to his palace a vexed and sullen man; he'd set his heart on that vineyard. He went to bed and sulked and wouldn't have anything to eat.

QUEEN   Why are you sulking?

NARRATOR   He told what had happened. She was a foreign princess, and was thinking of what her father, the King of Tyre, would have done.

QUEEN   You're a fine king. Get up and eat your food and stop worrying. I'll see you get the vineyard.

NARRATOR   She sent a royal letter sealed with the royal seal, to the aldermen and freemen of the city, all Naboth's fellow-councillors.

QUEEN   Proclaim a religious fast, and put Naboth where everybody can see him. Get two witnesses – you know what kind of men to get – to sit facing him and to charge him with cursing God and the king. You know what the sentence is – death by stoning.

NARRATOR   The city council carried out the royal orders to the letter. They held the fast, suborned the witnesses and had Naboth executed outside the city. They sent a brief report: 'Naboth has been executed.'

QUEEN	Get up and go down to the vineyard. It's yours now. Naboth wouldn't sell it to you would he? Well – he's dead!
NARRATOR	The king got up and went down to the vineyard to take possession of it. (By law the property of rebels and criminals became the king's.) God spoke to Elijah:
GOD	Get up and go and meet King Ahab face to face. He's in Naboth's vineyard; he's gone to take possession of it. Give him this message from me: 'You've committed murder to get hold of a vineyard. Where the street-dogs are licking up Naboth's blood, they'll one day lick up yours!'
KING	(*to Elijah*) Have you caught up with me, my enemy?
ELIJAH	I've caught up with you, all right. You've sold your soul in this foul deed; you've signed your own death-warrant – and that of your family. 'I'll get rid of you all!' says God.
NARRATOR	When King Ahab heard these words, he tore his robes and wore sackcloth. He accepted Elijah's rebuke.
Comment	King Ahab is shattered when he realises the evil his wife has led him into. He cries out to God in sorrow.

Prayer	*Psalm 130*
	From the depths I call to you, Lord,
	Lord, listen to my cry for help!
	Listen compassionately
	  to my pleading!
	
	If you never overlooked our sins, Lord,
	Lord, could anyone survive?
	But you do forgive us:
	  and for that we revere you.

Comment	Our song that follows reminds us that we too have failed in our relationship with God – but his message is as gentle as silence.
Song	'Oh, the love of my Lord', CH 231, FH I 79, FP 81, HON 195.

D28   God on Our Side

Comment

In modern times the Israeli army has proved itself to be one of the best in the world. In Old Testament times, the Israelites won many battles with God helping them. This one, during the revolt King Saul led against the Philistines, was won through the bravery of Jonathan, the king's son.

Reading

NARRATOR

Saul's troops numbered 600. He and Jonathan now set up camp at Gibeah. The Philistines held Michmash and sent out three raiding parties to capture strategic points in the highlands and the main body of the Philistines at Michmash pushed out an outpost to the heights above the Michmash Pass.

One day Jonathan spoke to his young armour-bearer.

JONATHAN

Let's go and have a look at the Philistine outpost over there on the other side of the pass.

NARRATOR

Saul had taken his stand, with his 600 soldiers, outside Gibeah where he had his headquarters under the pomegranate tree by the threshing-floor. Jonathan said nothing about his plans to his father; even the soldiers didn't know he had gone off.

Now on either side of the Michmash Pass there were two steep cliffs, one on each side, north and south (their local names were 'Slippery Rock' and 'Thorny Rock').

JONATHAN

Let's go over to these heathen Philistines. God will be on our side – he doesn't depend on numbers.

ARMOUR-
BEARER

Go ahead. I'm your man!

JONATHAN

Now listen. We'll let them see us. If they shout at us 'You stay where you are till we get at you!' we'll just stay put. But if they shout 'Come on up and try your luck!' then up we go. That's a sure sign God's put them at our mercy.

NARRATOR	They both stepped out and let themselves be seen.
PHILISTINE SENTRY	Look, the highlanders are coming out of their hide-outs!
NARRATOR	The sentries hailed the two men.
SENTRIES	Come on up, we'll show you a thing or two!
JONATHAN	After me, God's put them at our mercy!
NARRATOR	He scrambled up on his hands and knees, the soldier after him. They caught the sentries by surprise (they had no idea there was a path up the cliff). Jonathan knocked them down and his armour-bearer killed them off – twenty men on the narrow ledge.
	Panic spread throughout the Philistine camp – and beyond. There happened to be an earthquake just at that moment too; the Philistine army and the raiding columns were terrified and the panic became a rout.
	The Israelite look-outs in Gibeah were watching the Philistine camp and saw the soldiers suddenly scattering in all directions.
SAUL	Who's missing? Find out!
NARRATOR	Jonathan and his armour-bearer were missing at the roll-call. Saul and his men raced over to the fight. Everybody seemed to be fighting everybody else; it was complete chaos. Even the Israelites who had gone over to the Philistines and were serving with their army deserted and joined Saul and Jonathan. Men who had been hiding in the highlands came out and joined in the pursuit. So God rescued the Israelites that day.

Alan Dale, *Winding Quest*

Comment	Jonathan was very daring and brave to have taken on such odds but he was convinced of God's help. We too must remember, when things go badly, that God is at hand ready to help.
Prayer	*Psalm 44* O God, we ourselves have heard – our Fathers have told us – all you did in their days long ago:

uprooting and planting peoples,
hewing down and transplanting.
It wasn't our soldiers who conquered the country,
or our arms that won us the victory;
it was the strength of your hand and arm
the light of your face –
your good favour.
In God we will boast all the day,
to your name for ever give thanks!

Hymn   'At the name of Jesus', AM 225, CH 28, FH II 81, HON 27,
NL 136, SLW 45.

D29   Friendship with God

Opening record 'You've got a friend', James Taylor, WB 16085 (*fade after 1 min. 30 sec.*).

Comment   It's a great shame when people stop talking to God as a friend. Many learn to pray and do it quite naturally when they are young, but think it is childish and drop it as they get older. Listen to this wonderful closeness between Abraham and God; Abraham felt close enough to argue and bargain with God.

Reading

NARRATOR   God had told Abraham what he was going to do.

GOD   I have heard a cry for help against the two towns Sodom and Gomorrah. I must go down to see what it's all about. I must know if their conduct is what I think it is.

NARRATOR   The men went on down towards the town; Abraham remained standing in God's presence. They were on the high hills and the valleys lay all below them.

ABRAHAM   Would you sweep away the good people with the bad? Suppose there were fifty good people in the town, would you sweep it away – and not spare it for the sake of those fifty? I don't think you could do such a thing – treat good and bad alike. Must not the Judge of all the earth himself be just?

GOD	I will spare the whole town if I find fifty good people living there.
ABRAHAM	I am a mere man, and yet I dare to speak to you who are God. Suppose there aren't fifty; suppose there are five short? Will you sweep away the whole town just because there are five short?
GOD	If I find forty-five good people in the town, I won't sweep it away.
ABRAHAM	Suppose there are only forty?
GOD	For the sake of forty, I will not sweep the town away.
ABRAHAM	Don't be angry with me if I go on. Suppose the number is thirty?
GOD	I will not do it if I find thirty.
ABRAHAM	I am daring to speak again. Suppose there are only twenty?
GOD	I will not sweep the town away for the sake of those twenty.
ABRAHAM	Don't be angry with me for speaking again. Suppose only ten good people are to be found there?
GOD	For the sake of those ten, I will not sweep it away.
NARRATOR	God had no more to say and went on his way; Abraham went home.

Alan T. Dale, *Winding Quest*

Comment Jesus said 'Unless you become like little children, you shall not enter into heaven.' He meant that we should grow up, of course, but keep a simple trust and closeness to God our Father. Jesus taught us to think of God as a loving Father, with whom we can share all our worries and problems. God knows more about us than anyone else.

Reading I thank you for being what you are –
awe-inspiring, wonderful,
wonderful in all you do.
You made me the man I am
in the depth of my being;

> you've known what I am really like
> from the moment I was born.
> You have watched the marvel of my body,
> the wonder of my birth;
> you've seen me grow up
> and marked all I've done –
> no day passed by uncounted,
> slipped by unnoticed.
>
> What you think of me matters to me, O God,
> more than anything else –
> how much you know about me!
> I cannot fathom your thoughts
> any more than I can count the sand on the shore!
> Yet after all my searching
> I am still in your presence!

Alan T. Dale, Winding Quest

Comment   Remembering that we are now in God's presence let us say the prayer that Jesus himself taught us to say.

ALL   Our Father . . .

Hymn   'Walk with me', CH 340, FH II 2, FP 191, HON 292 *or replay opening record.*

D30   Trust

Opening record Theme music from *Star Wars*.

Comment   Did you see *Star Wars*? The heroes wished one another 'May the Force be with you.' In the film they had a clear idea that they couldn't beat the power of Vader – the power of evil – on their own, they needed the power of Good on their side.

   In the Bible God sometimes asks people to do difficult and dangerous things. He says to them 'I will be with you.'

Reading

NARRATOR   At Ophrah, in the Jezreel Plain, there was an oak tree.

It belonged to a man called Joash whose son was called
Gideon. The Midianites – camel-riding nomads from
the desert – were raiding the Hebrew villages.

Gideon was threshing wheat, but not openly on the
village threshing-floor. He was beating a few sheaves of
wheat down on the floor of the wine-press, to keep it
out of sight of the raiders. God spoke to him there.

GOD   God is with you, brave hero.

GIDEON   Then tell me, if God is on our side, why has there been
all this raiding?

GOD   You're a leader. Go and rescue your fellow countrymen
from the raiders. Am I not sending you?

GIDEON   Tell me, sir, how can I rescue my fellow countrymen?
We're the poorest clan in Manasseh; and I carry no
influence at all in my clan.

GOD   I will be on your side. You shall wipe out the raiders to
the last man.

GIDEON   Don't go away, I beg you. Wait here till I come back
with my present for you.

GOD   I'll stay till you come back.

NARRATOR   Gideon went inside. He prepared a kid-goat and made
unleavened cakes with some flour. He put the meat in a
basket and the broth in a pot. He brought them back to
the oak tree and offered his present to his visitor.

Gideon built an altar on the spot. He was filled with
God's Spirit and mustered his clan to follow him. They
got up early and set up camp near Harod Well. The
raider's camp lay to the north of them, by Teacher's
Hill in the valley of Jezreel.

That very night God spoke to him.

GOD   Get up and go down to the camp. It's yours. If you are
too scared to go alone, take your servant Purah with
you. Listen to the raiders talking. That will give you
courage enough to attack the camp.

NARRATOR   They both crept down to the camp and got close to the
tents of the outposts. A man was talking.

1ST RAIDER	I've just had a strange dream. I saw a loaf of barley bread come tumbling into the camp. It smashed a tent flat.
2ND RAIDER	I know what that means. It's Gideon's army. It means we're beaten.
NARRATOR	When Gideon heard that, he said a prayer to God and went back to his own men.
GIDEON	Up! God's giving the raiders into our hands!
NARRATOR	He divided his 300 men into three companies and gave them jars with torches inside.
GIDEON	Watch me. When we reach the tents, make sure you do just what I do. And when I blow the trumpet, shout 'For God and for Gideon!'
NARRATOR	They reached the camp about midnight, just after the guard had been changed. They surrounded it, smashed the jars with a loud noise, waved the torches in their left hands and held their swords in their right hands.
ALL	For God and for Gideon!
NARRATOR	The camp awoke and stampeded down the valley and over the Jordan. Gideon had only 300 men, but they followed the raiders across the Jordan and into the eastern highlands. He followed the caravan road and caught the raiders off their guard. The chieftains escaped. He went after them and caught them; and the raiding army melted away. He turned for home.

Alan T. Dale, *Winding Quest*

Comment	God is always with us, wherever we are. We can always ask him for help.

Prayer	*Psalm 121*
	God, guardian of his people,
	    is never drowsy or sleepy.
	God is your guardian at your side.
	    No harm shall come to you
	    from the sun in the daytime,
	    from the moon at night.

God will guard your whole life
from every danger –
when you go out, and when you come home,
from now on and for ever!

Record *Bring up theme music of* Star Wars *at end of prayer.*

D31 Vocation

Opening record 'Bannerman', Blue Mink, Regal RZ 3034.

Comment God has asked many people throughout time to be 'bannermen' or 'bannerwomen' – carrying God's message to others. They were often unpopular and felt unsuited to speak for God. But they knew that they had been called to a special task. This is the sort of answer they gave.

Reading 1

NARRATOR The boy Samuel was ministering to the Lord in the presence of Eli; it was rare for the Lord to speak in those days – visions were uncommon. One day, it happened that Eli was lying down in his room. His eyes were beginning to grow dim and he could no longer see. The lamp of God had not yet gone out and Samuel was lying in the sanctuary of the Lord where the ark of God was, when the Lord called,

GOD (*voice offstage*) Samuel! Samuel!

NARRATOR Samuel answered,

SAMUEL Here I am.

NARRATOR Samuel ran to Eli.

SAMUEL Here I am, since you called me.

ELI I did not call. Go back and lie down.

NARRATOR So he went and lay down. Once again the Lord called,

GOD Samuel! Samuel!

NARRATOR	Samuel got up and went to Eli.
SAMUEL	Here I am, since you called me.
ELI	I did not call you, my son; go back and lie down.
NARRATOR	Samuel had as yet no knowledge of the Lord, and the word of the Lord had not yet been revealed to him. Once again the Lord called, the third time.
GOD	Samuel! Samuel!
SAMUEL	(*to Eli*) Here I am, since you called me.
NARRATOR	Eli then understood that it was the Lord who was calling the boy.
ELI	Go and lie down, and if someone calls, say, 'Speak, Lord, your servant is listening.'
NARRATOR	So Samuel went and lay down in his place. The Lord then came, calling as he had done before,
GOD	Samuel! Samuel!
SAMUEL	Speak, Lord, your servant is listening.

1 Samuel 3:1–9 (*Jerusalem Bible*)

Comment	Samuel was surprised to be called by God. God often chooses the people we would least expect to work for him.
	Here is how Jeremiah the prophet remembered his calling by God.

Reading 2

JEREMIAH	The word of the Lord was addressed to me, saying,
GOD	(*voice offstage*) Before I formed you in the womb I knew you; before you came to birth I consecrated you; I have appointed you as prophet to the nations.
JEREMIAH	I said, 'Ah, Lord; look, I do not know how to speak; I am a child!'
GOD	Do not say, 'I am a child.' Go now to those to whom I send you and say whatever I command you.

Do not be afraid of them,
for I am with you to protect you –
it is the Lord who speaks!

JEREMIAH   Then the Lord put out his hand and touched my mouth
and said to me:

GOD   There! I am putting my words into your mouth.
Look, today I am setting you
over nations and over kingdoms,
to tear up and to knock down,
to destroy and to overthrow,
to build and to plant.

Jeremiah 1:4–10 (*Jerusalem Bible*)

Record   *Bring up 'Bannerman' for a minute and then fade.*

Prayer   Almighty Father, I wish I could be like Samuel and hear
you speaking to me. When I say my prayers I get no
answer. I never hear your voice. You never call me to
do anything. I'm not even sure that you hear my
prayers. Make my faith and trust deeper that I may
come closer to you. May I be always open to your will
for me – just show me what it is. Amen.

D32   Respect for Authority

Opening record 'Bridge over troubled waters', Simon & Garfunkel, CBS
4790 *(fade after 1 min. 30 sec.)*.

Comment   When two people are at 'loggerheads' it sometimes
requires one to make the first move – to offer friendship
or make some gesture of respect and regard. David did
that when Saul was hunting to kill him.

Reading

NARRATOR   The people of Ziph took the news that David was
hiding near them to Saul in Gibeah. He called out his
crack troops and marched to the wilderness of Ziph to
hunt him out. He pitched camp on Hachilah Hill on the
road facing 'the Desert'.

David was out in the rough moorlands when he heard that Saul was tracking him down. He sent scouts to find out where he was.

Then he moved quickly. He marched by night to the outskirts of Saul's camp. Saul and his commander-in-chief, Abner, were asleep – Saul lying in the trench, the soldiers in their tents round him as a guard.

David called two men, the Hittite Ahimelech, and Abishai.

DAVID   Which of you will go down with me to the camp – to Saul?

ABISHAI   I will.

NARRATOR   So, through the darkness, the two men stole down to the camp. There was Saul lying asleep in the trench – his spear stuck in the ground at his head, Abner and the soldiers lying round him.

ABISHAI   God has put your enemy at your mercy. I'll pin him to the earth with his own spear. One stroke's enough.

DAVID   No murder. Saul is God's anointed king – murder of God's anointed king is a dreadful thing. In God's name, no murder! We'll leave him in God's hands, to die an ordinary death or meet a soldier's violent end. But God forbid that I should lay my hand on his anointed king. Get the spear at his head, and the water-jug there – and let's get out!

NARRATOR   So they took the spear and the water-jug from near Saul's head and slipped away. Nobody saw or heard them, and nobody woke up. They were all sound asleep. David crossed the valley and stood at a safe distance on a hilltop on the other side. He was so far off that he had to shout as loud as he could to be heard.

DAVID   Why don't you answer, Abner?

ABNER   Who are you, calling up the king like this?

DAVID   You're a fine soldier. You're the finest soldier of them all. What sort of guard is this to keep over his majesty the king? Didn't you know there's an assassin prowling round? What a soldier you are! By God, you ought to be executed for sleeping – you're supposed to be on guard, you know! Do you want proof? See where the king's spear and his water-jug are now – not at his head!

NARRATOR   Saul, awake by now, recognised David's voice.

SAUL   Is that you, my son David?

DAVID   It is, your majesty. And let me finish what I have to say. Why do you hunt me like this? What have I done wrong? If God's made you do this, let us ask his forgiveness; but if it's just slander, God's curse be on the slanderers – they have driven me out of the fellowship of God's people and tried to make me a foreigner. Don't let my blood be spilt in this foreign countryside. You're hunting me like a hawk hunting a partridge in the highlands!

SAUL   I'm in the wrong. Come back to me, my son David. I'll do you no more hurt; you treated me as the real king today. I've been a fool and done a dreadful thing.

DAVID   The king's spear is here. Let one of the soldiers come over and fetch it.

SAUL   God bless you, my son David. You've a great future in front of you!

NARRATOR   David went on his way and Saul went home.

Alan T. Dale, *Winding Quest*

Comment   David could so easily have killed Saul the man who had been hunting him, but he had too great a respect for authority. Those who are in authority, whether it is in government, the police, school or home should remember that all authority springs from God. And God exercises his authority in loving care.

In the psalm of thanksgiving that follows, please reply 'His love is everlasting' to each of the reader's invocations.

Prayer   *Psalm 136*

READER   Give thanks to the Lord, for he is good.

ALL   His love is everlasting!

READER	Give thanks to the God of gods.
ALL	His love is everlasting!
READER	Give thanks to the Lord of lords.
ALL	His love is everlasting!
READER	He alone performs great marvels.
ALL	His love is everlasting!
READER	His wisdom made the heavens.
ALL	His love is everlasting!
READER	He set the earth on the waters.
ALL	His love is everlasting!
READER	He made the great lights.
ALL	His love is everlasting!
READER	The sun to govern the day.
ALL	His love is everlasting!
READER	Moon and stars to govern the night.
ALL	His love is everlasting!
READER	He provides for all living creatures.
ALL	His love is everlasting!
READER	Give thanks to the God of Heaven.
ALL	His love is everlasting!
Hymn	'Praise my soul', AM 365, CH 260, HON 223, NL 58, PL 95, *or replay opening record.*

D33   Forgiveness

Opening record Joseph and his Amazing Technicolour Dreamcoat, Decca SKL 4973, *side one, track one (fade after 1 min. 40 sec.).*

Reading

NARRATOR	Joseph was 17 years old. His father had been quite an old man when he was born, and he had always openly treated him as his favourite son. He made him a princely coat (a coat with long sleeves) to wear. His brothers resented all this; they hadn't a kind word to say to him.
	Now Joseph used to dream and he could not keep his dreams to himself. This too upset his brothers.
	The time came for the brothers to lead the flocks away to the north to Shechem, to summer pastures. The grass was more abundant there than around Hebron.
	His father spoke to Joseph one day.
JACOB	Your brothers are away in the highlands. I want you to go and visit them for me.
JOSEPH	All right.
JACOB	See how they and the sheep are getting on and bring me any news.
NARRATOR	Joseph found his brothers near Dothan, an ancient Canaanite city. They saw him coming. Here was their chance to get their own back. By the time he'd got up to them, they'd made up their minds.
BROTHERS (*together*)	Here comes the dreamer! Let's get rid of him and throw his body into one of these rain-pits. We can make up a story about his being eaten by a wild animal. We'll make his dreams come true all right!
REUBEN	Let's have no murder. Throw him into one of these rain-pits, if you want, but keep your hands off him.
NARRATOR	He intended to come back and get him out of the pit and take him home.
	They threw him into one of the empty rain-pits.
	Quite by chance, some Midianite traders passed by. They pulled the boy out of the pit and took him off to Egypt with them.
	Reuben came back to the pit – but there was no Joseph in it. He tore his clothes in grief and ran back to his brothers.

REUBEN	The lad's gone! And now what am I to do? How can I go home?
NARRATOR	The brothers had taken Joseph's fine long-sleeved coat off him before they threw him into the pit. They tore it up and took it home with them to their father.
BROTHERS	We found this. Can you recognise it?
JACOB	It's my son's cloak! A wild animal's mauled him. He must have been torn to pieces!
NARRATOR	In his grief, Jacob tore his clothes and put sackcloth on. He broke down in tears.
Comment	Joseph, you remember, after being a servant for a short time, found himself in prison. He got out of prison by being able to interpret the Pharaoh's dreams. The Pharaoh was so grateful that he made Joseph his second-in-command in Egypt. Famine struck his family's homeland and the brothers came to Egypt begging for grain.
Record *(optional)*	*Joseph and the Amazing Technicolour Dreamcoat (last 2 mins. 45 sec. of side one).*
Comment	Joseph was released from prison when he successfully interpreted the Pharaoh's dreams. After playing a few tricks on the brothers, Joseph told them who he was.

Reading

NARRATOR	Joseph could hold back his feelings no longer. He ordered all officials out of the audience room. Then he broke down – everybody in the palace could hear his weeping.
JOSEPH	Come near to me.
NARRATOR	The brothers gathered round him.
JOSEPH	I am your brother Joseph. Now don't be angry with yourselves for what you did. There are five more years of famine ahead of us; God sent me here so that our family might survive. You must go back home with this message from me to my father: 'God has made me

Viceroy of Egypt. Make haste and come down to me. You can live in the land of Goshen, near me – you and the whole clan with your flocks and possessions. I will look after you and see that you don't starve.'

Alan T. Dale, Winding Quest

Comment What do we learn from this story? There are many lessons but one is the willingness to forgive. Joseph forgave his brothers for trying to kill him, and for the years he'd spent in prison. He bore no grudge.

Record *Joseph and the Amazing Technicolour Dreamcoat (side two, last 2½ min., fade).*

D34 Doing God's Will

Opening record 'Sailing', Rod Stewart, WB 16000 *(fade after 1 min.)*.

Comment The usual way to sail is in a boat, but Jonah in the Old Testament found himself travelling in a great sea beast. (Many people believe that the story you are about to hear was made up to teach a truth – that God cares about everyone. Jonah, a Jew, did not want to go and talk to non-Jews – but God insisted!)

Reading

NARRATOR Once upon a time God spoke to Jonah.

GOD Get up, and go to that great city, Nineveh. Pronounce its doom – its shameful wickedness has been reported to me.

NARRATOR Jonah set off – but he made for Tartessus in the far west, right away from God. He went down to the port of Joppa. There was a large cargo boat in the harbour. He paid his passage and went on board; he didn't want to have anything to do with God and his commands.

Out at sea they ran into a hurricane. The sea was so rough that the ship seemed about to break up. The sailors were in a panic, each shouting out to his own

God for help. They threw the cargo overboard to lighten the ship.

Jonah had gone down into the hold, and was lying there fast asleep. The captain went down to see what he was doing.

CAPTAIN   What do you mean by sleeping like this? Get up and pray to your God. He might take some notice of us and come to our help.

NARRATOR   Meanwhile the sailors were talking together.

1st SAILOR   Let's toss up, and find out who's to blame for this bad luck.

NARRATOR   They tossed up – it was Jonah!

2nd SAILOR   Tell us your business, where do you come from? What's your country? Who are your people?

JONAH   I'm a Hebrew. I'm running away from God – the God of heaven who made the sea and the land.

1st SAILOR   What a thing to do. What shall we do with you to quieten the storm?

NARRATOR   The sea was growing rougher and rougher.

JONAH   Throw me overboard. That will calm the sea. I know I am to blame for this hurricane.

NARRATOR   But the men didn't throw him overboard. They rowed as hard as they could to get the ship into harbour. All in vain – the sea grew stormier and stormier still. Then they prayed to Jonah's God:

SAILORS   O God, don't let us die if we throw this man overboard; don't hold it against us. The storm is your doing.

NARRATOR   Then they threw Jonah overboard – and the storm died down.

The sailors were filled with awe in God's presence; they worshipped him and vowed to serve him.

God sent a great fish. It swallowed Jonah, and there he stayed, inside the fish, for three whole days. He then ordered the fish to put Jonah on shore, and it vomited him out on to the dry land.

Alan T. Dale, *Winding Quest*

Comment   The Bible story says that the storm arose because Jonah
was going off in the opposite direction to the one God
wanted him to take – he was running away from doing
what God had asked. Eventually Jonah did as he was
told.

Prayer   *Psalm 145*
I sing your praises, God my King,
I bless your name for ever and ever,
blessing you day after day,
and praising your name for ever and ever.

Always true to his promises,
the Lord shows love in all he does.
Only stumble, and the Lord at once supports you,
if others bow you down, he will raise you up.

The Lord's praise be ever in my mouth,
and let every creature bless his holy name
for ever and ever.

Hymn   'Praise we our God with joy', CH 266, HON 228, PL 94,
or replay opening record.

D35   God's Covenant

Opening record 'By the rivers of Babylon', Boney M, Atlantic K 11120
(fade after 1 min. 30 sec.).

Comment   Powerful armies swept in from the north and over-ran
the Jewish people and thousands of them were taken
away into exile in Babylon. This exile had been
threatened by the prophets because the Jews had failed
to follow God's way.

Reading   In the days that are to be,
    God says,
I will make a new covenant
    with both North and South.

It won't be like the old covenant
    I made on the desert march

when I led your ancestors
   out of Egypt.
That covenant was broken long ago –
   that's why I said No to them.

This is the new covenant
   I will make with the whole people:
My Way shall be clear to everybody's conscience,
   something every man can recognise;
I will really be their God,
   they shall really be my people.

There'll be no need for teachers,
   for anybody to say
'Live in God's Way'
   to neighbour or brother.
Each shall know for himself
   what my Way is –
humble peasant
   and King on his throne alike,
      says God.

I'll forgive them
   the wrong they've done –
their disloyalty
   shall be a thing of the past.

Alan T. Dale, *Winding Quest*

Comment   God did make a new covenant with his people, but not before the Jews had suffered much unhappiness and had even been asked to sing their own religious songs for their guards.

Reading   *Psalm 137*
Beside the streams of Babylon
we sat and wept
at the memory of Zion,
leaving our harps hanging on the poplars there.

For we had been asked
to sing to our captors,
to entertain those who had carried us off:
'sing' they said
'some hymns of Zion.'

How could we sing
one of the Lord's hymns
in a pagan country?
Jerusalem, if I forget you,
may my right hand wither!

Record   'By the rivers of Babylon' *(the remainder of the record)*.

Comment   The agreement, or covenant, that God made with his People prepared a way for the coming of Christ. Jesus himself gave us a covenant – a new and lasting agreement.

Reading   While they were at supper Jesus took some bread, and when he had given thanks, broke it and gave it to them saying, 'This is my body which will be given for you; do this as a memorial of me.' He did the same with the cup after supper, and said, 'This cup is the new covenant in my blood which will be poured out for you.'

Luke 22:19–20

(Short period of silence)

Hymn   'Love is his word', CH 185, FH I 66, FP 107, HON 166, PL 75, *or replay opening record.*

World Religious Themes

E36   Creation

Opening record Holst, *The Planets* (*suitable short extract*).

Comment   That piece of music is taken from *The Planets* by Holst. These days, when pictures are sent hundreds of millions of miles back in space by space probes from other planets in our solar system, it is natural to ask how this planet – Earth – got here. This question – where did Earth come from – has always puzzled man. All the religions of the world have stories about creation. Here are three.

READER A   The holy men of ancient India often wondered how the Universe was made. They were specially puzzled about how Creation began. The first reading is from a book called *The Laws of Manu*.

The Universe we live in was like darkness:
Unnoticed, difficult to recognise, impossible
To understand; beyond knowledge;
Like someone who is far away, or fast asleep.

Then he himself appeared, divine,
Impossible to recognise:
The one who made it all –
The great things and the little things
    that we can know, and learn about.
He himself appeared, with power you can't resist:
Power to create.
He came, and the darkness faded away.

Laws of Manu 1.5.16

READER B   The second reading is from the Muslim holy book, the *Qur'an*.

God is He who created the heavens and the earth and

sent down water from the clouds, then brought forth
with it the fruits as a sustenance for you, and He has
made subservient to you the sun and the moon pursu-
ing their courses, and He has made subservient to you
the night and the day. And he gives you all that you ask
Him, and if you count God's favours, you will not be
able to number them; surely man is very unjust, very
ungrateful.

The Qur'an

READER C   The Jewish people too had their stories of creation.
This is the first of the two that appear in the Bible. It is
imagined how God spread the work of creation over
seven days; here is a little of it.

This is the story of the making
    of earth and sky:
in the very beginning,
    God made them both.

Earth was formless chaos
    lost in darkness
with stormy winds
    sweeping over the vast waters.
'Let there be light!' said God –
and everywhere there was light,
    splendid in his eyes.
He marked off light from darkness,
    calling light 'day'
and darkness 'night':
    so came the evening and the morning
of the first day.

Alan T. Dale, *Winding Quest*

Comment   These are religious ways of trying to understand that
tremendous event – the beginning of life on planet
earth. A modern poet tries to put the same ideas into
the language of our day.

READER D   And God stepped out on space,
And he looked around and said:
I'm lonely . . . .
I'll make me a world.

As far as the eye of God could see
Darkness covered everything
Blacker than a hundred midnights
Down in a cypress swamp.
Then God smiled
And the light broke,
And the darkness rolled up on one side,
And the light stood shining on the other,
And God said: 'That's good!'

James Weldon Johnson, *The Creation*

Comment   If you look into space on a clear night, and start to think about how far away the stars are; how many points of light you can see, whether space has an ending to it and so on. Then you begin to realise the sheer vastness of it all. And the mighty power of God. We are so small before so great a wonder.

Song   'Morning has broken', CH 196, FH I 73, FP 196, HON 171, NL 79, SLW 9.

E37   Supreme Being

Background music   Beethoven, *Symphony No. 6* ('*Pastoral*'), Philips 6580050 (*short extract*).

Reading 1
O God our king
   how majestic you are!
Your glory is in the earth,
   your splendour in the skies!
When I gaze at the sky
   your fingers formed,
the moon and the stars
   you have set there –
'What is man,' I cry,
   'that you should notice him,
mortal man,
   that you should care about him?'

Psalm 8

Comment	The idea of God – the Supreme Being – is common to most religions. He is mighty and powerful; the creator – as the Jews understood. The reading we have just heard is from one of their psalms in the Bible. God has no beginning and no end – as the Muslim faith reminds us.
Reading 2	'Say: God is one The eternal God He begets not nor is he begotten And there is none like him.'
Comment	The Qur'an also states: 'Say you: we believe in God and in that which has been sent down on us and sent down on Abraham, Ishmael, Isaac and Jacob and the tribes, and that which was given to Moses and Jesus and the prophets of the Lord. We make no division between any of them and to him we surrender.' <div align="right">Riadh El Droubie</div>
Comment	For Hindus there are many gods but . . .
Reading 3	'Whichever god you pray to, it is I who answer the prayer', says Krishna, who combines the concept of God and the Absolute. 'As different streams, having different sources, all find their way to the sea, so, O Lord, the different paths which men take all lead to thee.'
Comment	A modern poet reminds us that the awesome mystery of God is not only far above and beyond this world, but also within it.
Reading 4	The emeralds are singing on the grasses and in the trees the bells of the long cold are ringing. My blood seems changed to emeralds like the spears of grass beneath the earth piercing and singing. The flame of the first blade Is an angel piercing through the earth to sing 'GOD is everything!' The grass within the grass, the angel in the angel, flame Within the flame, and He is the green shade that came

To be the heart of shade.
The grey-beard angel of the stone,
Who has grown wise with age, cried 'Not alone
Am I within my silence – God is the stone in the still
stone,
the silence laid
In the heart of silence . . . then, above the glade the
yellow
straws of light whereof the sun has built his nest, cry,
'Bright is the world, the yellow straw
My brother – God is the straw within the straw:–
All things are Light.'

He is the sea of ripeness and the sweet apple's emerald
lore.
So you, my flame of grass, my root of the world from
which
all spring shall grow,
O you, my hawthorn bough of the stars, now leaning
low
Through the day, for your flowers to kiss my lips,
Shall know
He is the core of the heart of love and he, beyond
labouring seas, our ultimate shore.

Edith Sitwell, *How many Heavens*

Record   'My sweet Lord', George Harrison, Apple R 5884.

or

Hymn   'O Lord by God', CH 227, FH II 27, FP 8, HON 202, *or*
'Dear Lord and Father of Mankind', AM 184, CH 60,
HON 55, PL 100.

E38   Worship

Opening record 'Day by day', Holly Sherwood, Bell 1182 *(fade)*.

Comment   That record came from the musical *Godspell*. It sums
up the attitude of Jesus's friends towards him. Prayer
and worship did not begin with Jesus, but go back beyond

the beginning of recorded history. Men and women of all ages have believed that if there is a Supreme Being then we owe him respect and worship.

This is how a pagan Roman prayed.

READER A   In his famous story of Rome, the Latin writer Livy tells how the Admiral of the Roman Fleet, Scipio Africanus, prayed as he prepared to attack the North African city of Carthage, in 204 BC.

I pray to all the gods and goddesses
Who live on land or in the sea,
I pray you, with all my heart,
That what men have done already, under my orders,
Will help me.

Give us the power to take revenge on our enemies:
Give to me, and to the Roman people,
The power to do to Carthage
What they planned to do to us;
Show them what it means to suffer punishment from God.

Donald G. Butler, *Many Lights*

Comment   Let us look at the attitude of world faiths to worship and prayer. The Christian attitude to prayer can be seen in this reading from the rules St Benedict put together for his monks.

READER B   When we make requests to men in high positions,
We would not dare to do so without
Respect and politeness;
Even more, then, we should pray to God,
The Lord of All,
With politeness, and devout sincerity in our hearts.
We must realise that our prayers will be heard,
Not if we just pray, over and over again,
But if we are really sincere,
And really sorry for our sins.
So prayers ought to be short and sincere
(Unless we are really inspired to pray longer).

Donald G. Butler, *Many Lights*

Comment	The Hindu approach to prayer is summed up in these words from the Bhagavad-gita.
READER C	Fix your thoughts on me, Worship me, make offerings to me, Go down on your knee to me: That is the way to get to know me. Be sure of this: I promise: I will not disappoint you: You mean so much to me.

Donald G. Butler, Many Lights

Comment	Prayer should be regular, as well as respectful. Regular daily prayer is an essential part of the Muslim faith.

READER D	From the sacred book of Islam, the Qur'an, comes these instructions about the right way for Muslims to say their daily prayers:
	
	The five hours of prayer are
	    In the early morning with a reading from the holy Qur'an;
	    immediately the sun begins to go down, after midday;
	    in the late afternoon;
	    immediately after sunset;
	    after the sun has set, and darkness has set in.

Donald G. Butler, Many Lights

Comment	Let us listen to and make our own the words of this song.
Record	*As for opening.*

E39   Prayer

Comment	Newspaper headline, *Daily Mail*, 11 August 1979: 'Baboo, a man of peace who was kicked to death.'
READER A	He was known as Baboo to his friends – easier to handle than Kayumarz Anklesaria, which even to his Pakistani

compatriots was something of a mouthful.

Everyone who knew him has stories to tell about Baboo. They are all affectionate. For all are agreed he was the most gentle of men.

Yesterday Baboo was dead – the victim of a vicious, totally unprovoked, and possibly racially-inspired attack on the London Underground.

He had left his home in Skelton Road, Forest Gate, London E., at 4.45 pm on Thursday and gone by bus and Tube to a temple in West Hampstead to meditate and pray. At 11.53 pm as the train rolled into Bromley-by-Bow station, three white youths wearing brown lace-up 'bovver' boots moved towards the doors. Suddenly, without any kind of warning, one delivered a savage Kung Fu-style kick at the Asian's neck. They ran out as the doors closed, laughing and shouting, and the train started to move.

Immediately a passenger pulled the emergency stop handle and the Tube jolted to a halt, still within the station. A group of nurses travelling on the train tried to make the injured man comfortable before an ambulance arrived to rush him to St Andrew's Hospital in Bow.

Baboo died of a smashed wind-pipe within half an hour of admittance.

Every week, as a devout Zoroastrian, he would travel across London to a converted temple in Compayne Gardens, West Hampstead. There he would burn sandalwood powder, and, kneeling before an open fire – the symbol of purity – he would pray to his god, Ahura Mazda, for peace, the love of his fellow man and for a world free of cruelty and violence.

In 1963, at the time of the Skopje earthquake in Yugoslavia in which thousands died, Baboo joined a volunteer organisation and, with only a sleeping-bag, went to help the refugees. He dug bodies from the rubble, helped the sick and injured. That, say his friends, was the kind of man he was.

Comment   A lot of you probably think that saying prayers is stuff for kids and young children, but not mature adults. Baboo doesn't sound like an immature adult – but the sixteen-year-old that killed him certainly could not be called a mature, balanced person.

Record   'A child's prayer', Hot Chocolate, RAK 221.

Comment   Children of the world's principal faiths learn to pray.

READER B   These are two of the prayers that Jewish children say when they go to bed.

We bless you, Lord God, King of the Universe:
You draw the garments of sleep over my eyes,
You give my eyelids their gentle slumber.
May it please you, my Lord and God, the God of my
     family,
To allow me to go to rest in peace,
And to rise again tomorrow in peace.

We bless the Lord by day:
We bless the Lord by night;
We bless the Lord when we go to bed:
We bless the Lord when we wake up.

Donald G. Butler, *Many Lights*

Comment   Sikh children learn to pray for those things which will help them most to live the life of a good Sikh.

READER C   God, grant me this prayer:
May I never turn away from the chance of doing good
     deeds.
May I never be afraid when I have to fight adversity.
May I never lose control when I win a victory.

I want, always, to have control over my heart:
This is what I want most from your goodness.

When the time finally comes for my life to find its end,
May I die in the thick of battles such as these.

Guru Gobind Singh, from Donald G. Butler, *Many Lights*

Comment   The family prayer of the Christian family is the Lord's Prayer. Listen to this new translation.

READER D   Father in heaven
We praise you: we hold your honour in great respect.

You are our king
And you will be king in all the world.
Everyone here on earth will serve you,
As they do in heaven.
Give us day by day the food we need;
Forgive the things that we do wrong,
As we forgive each other.
Help us when we are tempted to displease you;
Protect us from every kind of evil power.
You are our king, powerful and glorious,
Now and for ever.

Donald G. Butler, *Many Lights*

Record   *Replay* 'A child's prayer', Hot Chocolate, RAK 221.

E40   Fasting

Opening record 'Matchstalk men and matchstalk cats and dogs', Brian and Michael, Pye 7N 46035 *(fade after 1 min. 30 sec.)*.

Comment   The artist Lowry painted people to look like matchstick men. There are people who make themselves into matchstick figures. We've all seen newspaper headlines 'Girl fasts herself to death for a bet'. It is not uncommon to read stories in the papers of teenage girls and young women being so concerned to lose weight that they take slimming to dangerous extremes. They end up with a disease called anorexia. This is an inability to eat and can finally result in the person dying of malnutrition.

READER A   Abstention from food and drink on special occasions is practised for religious purposes too. Many religions encourage their members to go without food and drink on special fast days and in preparation for religious festivals. In this way they remind their members that there is more to life than material things – like food and drink. We have a spiritual side to us as well.

Anon.

Comment

The Jews observe total fasting on their special day, the Day of Atonement; that is from sunset to sunset. The Muslims fast for a whole month. Let us listen to this account of the Muslim fast as kept in the Arab State of Kuwait.

READER B

The fast of Ramadhan begins with the sightseeing of the new moon after the sun goes down. The fast of Ramadhan is strictly observed in Kuwait and greatly affects the daily life of every Muslim and even non-Muslims. The fasting begins early in the morning when the 'white thread of day' appears on the horizon and ends at sunset, when people can eat as much as they wish until early next morning. In the morning they fast again. During Ramadhan Muslims may not drink, eat or smoke during daylight hours and this routine affects foreign Muslims and non-Muslims, who are expected out of politeness to refrain from smoking, drinking and eating in public.

Mgr. V. Sanmiguel, *Pastor In Kuwait*

Comment

From the very early days of Christianity, following the example of Jesus, who went out into the desert to fast, the Christian Church has always encouraged its members to abstain from food and drink, especially in preparation for the festivals of Christmas and Easter.

READER C

The Christian concept of fasting is somewhat different from that of the Muslims. The Muslims, during the Ramadhan, between sunset and sunrise are freely allowed to eat in quantity and quality according to their will. While Christians during Lent and other fasting days, in imitation of the fast of Christ in the desert, abstain themselves throughout the fasting in quantity and quality meditating on the Passion of Christ.

The purpose of the fasting, besides the sacrifice, is to moderate the sensual passions and general submission of the material to the spiritual and moral sphere of the life of man. This rule is good not only for those who profess the religious life, but also for the ordinary good Christian.

Comment	Fasting, for a religious purpose, is of no value unless it is aimed at a growing in love for God and our neighbour.
Closing record or	'All you need is love', Beatles, Parlophone R 5620
Hymn	'Love is his word', CH 185, FH I 66, FP 107, HON 166, PL 75.

E41   The Golden Rule

Opening record	'Love is like oxygen', Sweet, Polydor POSP 1, *or* 'All you need is love', Beatles, Parlophone R5620.
Comment	From time to time we are reminded by a pop group, or in a new slogan, that love is necessary for life, like oxygen. That is something that the religions of the world have been teaching for a very long time. It's called the Golden Rule.
READER A	Jews and Christians, throughout the centuries, have not always been friends. Here is a story of the Golden Rule in action.
	The Grand Rabbi of Lyons was a Jewish chaplain to the French force in the 1914–18 war. One day a wounded man staggered into a trench and told the Rabbi that a Roman Catholic was on the point of death in no-man's-land and was begging that his padre should come to him with a crucifix. The padre could not quickly be found. The Jew rapidly improvised a cross, ran out with it into no-man's-land and was seen to hold it before the dying man's eyes. He was almost immediately shot by a sniper; the bodies of the Catholic and the Jew were found together.
	Victor Gollancz
Comment	For hundreds of years Sikhs and Muslims have been enemies; with only a few to remind them of the Golden Rule.

READER B   During a battle between Muslims and Sikhs, a Sikh
              water carrier called Ghanaya was seen giving water to
              wounded Muslim soldiers as they lay suffering from
              thirst under the hot sun. He was brought to Guru
              Gobind Singh and accused of being a traitor. The Guru
              heard the charges and asked Ghanaya to answer them.
              'When I walked through the battle fields I saw no
              Muslims and no Sikhs, only your face in every man',
              said Ghanaya. 'You are a true Sikh', said the Guru.
              'Continue the work; and here is some ointment to put
              on the wounds. You shall be known as Bhai Ghanaya
              from now on.' Bhai means brother; it is a term of
              honour among Sikhs, reserved for the best of men.

                                                     W. Owen Cole

Comment   It is interesting how close in thought the major religions
              of the world are when it comes to the wording of the
              Golden Rule, to be found in their teaching.

READER A   The Hindu religion says – 'The true rule is to guard and
              do by the things of others as you do by your own.'

READER B   The Muslim faith says – 'Let none of you treat your
              brother in a way he himself would dislike to be treated.'

READER C   The Buddhist religion says – 'One should seek for
              others the happiness one desires for oneself.'

READER D   Jesus summed it up for the Christian, telling his follow-
              ers, to 'Love one another as I have loved you.'

Comment   Let us close with the song which was specially written
              for Christian Aid, a fund which raises money by Christ-
              ians for their neighbours in the world who are poor and
              needy, no matter what their creed.

Hymn   'When I needed a neighbour', CH 353, FH I 41, NL 123,
              NO 13, PL 298.

E42 Festival of Light

Comment   Have you heard the story from a science class of when
the teacher told the class about the fantastic speed at
which light travels. 'Isn't it wonderful', said the
teacher, 'to think of light coming to us from the sun at
the speed of all those miles per second?' 'Not really',
said one boy, 'it's downhill all the way!' Of course light
from the sun is essential to life on this planet – no
sunlight, no life! Some world religions celebrate the
importance of light and use it as a symbol in worship.

READER A   The Jewish people have a special festival called
'Hanukkah' which means 'dedication'. They celebrate
on that day the rededication of their temple in the year
165 BC. The Romans had allowed a Syrian king to turn
the Jewish temple into a pagan place. A guerrilla leader
called Judas Maccabee organised a revolt and he won
back the Temple. Judas Maccabee wanted to light a
lamp as a sign of God's presence and love. All the lamps
had been spoiled but one. This only had enough oil in it
for one day, but Judas lit it and was surprised when it
burned for eight days. The Festival of Hanukkah lasts
for eight days and, on a special eight-branched candle-
stick, one candle is lit every day.

READER B   The Hindu religion has the 'Feast of Lamps' or Diwali,
when candles are lit in the window of each Hindu
house. The festival lasts for three days, and houses have
to be made clean and spotless. The light burning in
each house, and the bigger fires built on the third day
are to remind the Hindus – as they start a new year –
that as light overcomes darkness all men are to struggle
to overcome evil.

Comment   Christianity also uses light as a symbol.

READER C   The newly baptised child or adult is given a lighted
candle at the end of the Baptism service. This is to
remind them that now they too, like Christ, must be a
light in the world.

READER D   The Easter Candle is blessed at the Easter service called the Easter Vigil and stands in a prominent place in the church near the altar. This is to remind everyone that Christ is alive and risen.

Comment   (*Showing poster* PT 24) Whatever our religion we should always, as the poster reminds us, 'Walk in the Light'. (*or Argus poster* 42671, 'You are the light of the World').

E43   Judgement

Opening record 'Bright Eyes', Art Garfunkel, CBS 6947 (*fade after 1 min.*).

Comment   All of you must have seen at some time or other on TV the old films, *The Mummy* or *The Mummy's Curse*. Stories about finding secret passages and vaults in the pyramids and the burial riches of Pharaohs, like Tutankhamun. Later in the story comes the effect of the legendary curse of the Pharaohs on those who tampered with their tombs. The tombs were filled with treasures because the ancient Egyptians believed in a life after death. Their family and friends thought they would need all sorts of things in the next life. The Egyptians believed in many gods, but they believed a man's soul was sent for judgement and his life was examined. He was rewarded or punished according to how he'd lived.

READER A   I believe with all my heart,
              That God knows everything that
              His children do,
              Everything that they think.
              As it says: He made all their hearts,
              He knows all their deeds.

              I believe with all my heart,
              That God
              Rewards those who keep his Laws.

And punishes those who break them.

Donald G. Butler, *Many Lights*

Comment   Muslims too believe that there will be a judgement.

READER B   When a man dies, Muslims believe that he must undergo judgement. He may be condemned to hell or rewarded with heaven. Or he may be a very special person, and have a place very near to Allah's throne.

When the event inevitable
Cometh to pass
Then will no soul
Entertain falsehood
Concerning its coming.
Many will it bring low;
Many will it exalt.

Donald G. Butler, *Many Lights*

Comment   When Hazel of *Watership Down* dies, the story says he goes to his reward with the rabbits' god. He had lived a good life so presumably he was going to live for ever in happiness. I wonder what happened to General Woundwort at death? Christian belief in judgement at death is summed up in a short poem, written over 1,200 years ago by Bede, an Anglo-Saxon scholar.

Record   *Play part of* 'Bright Eyes' *again*.

READER C   There is a journey ahead
For everyone of us.

Before we begin that journey
We must, each one of us
(And none of us is so wise
That he can be left out),
Think out, in good time,

What judgement his soul will get
After death.
Will it be a judgement of evil?
Or a judgement of good?

Donald G. Butler, *Many Lights*

E44   Heaven

Comment   Have you ever dreamt of digging up buried treasure? People with metal detectors have made many finds – hoards of coins and jewellery, for example. Lots of things have been dug up in the past. Not just chests of coins and jewellery but important historical finds – archaeological finds that help us to piece together how people lived in the past. What they believed in has also come to light in the same way.

READER A   The following poem was found on an earthen tablet about thirty years ago by archaeologists excavating the ancient city of Babylon. It was very weathered and damaged.

READER B   There stands a house under the mountain of the world,
a road runs down, the mountain covers it
and no man knows the way. It is a house
that binds bad men with ropes
and clamps them into a narrow space.
It is a house that separates the wicked
and the good; this is a house from out of which
no one escapes, but just men need not fear before its judge,
for in this river of spent souls the good
shall never die although the wicked perish.

Comment   Those thoughts were put on the tablet about 600 years before Christ. That is over 2,500 years ago. Notice how the poet says 'the good shall never die'. The beliefs of Christians and Muslims continued and gave more meaning and depth to the idea of heaven.

READER C   Christians and Muslims affirm that there exists an Abode of Reward, Paradise, and an Abode of Punishment, Hell, though they differ widely in the descriptions they give of these places and in their understanding of what constitutes their essential elements. Does not Jesus announce in the Gospel that 'those who did good will rise again to life; and those who did evil to condemnation' (John 5:28–9)? Islamic tradition recognises the existence of 'pleasures of the mind and the senses', often interpreted metaphorically, and would seem to confine the 'vision of God' to a few rare moments and to the 'nearest amongst the elect'.

Mgr. Victor Sanmiguel, *Pastor in Kuwait*

E45   Happy New Year

Preparations   *Five posters or placards are made with the following dates on one side and the religion on the other. They are carried by five pupils who stand up and show their poster as the content is mentioned – first the side with the name of the world faith then the side with the date on.*

27 August	Zoroastrian New Year
13/14 September	Jewish New Year
11 November	Hindu New Year
Last Sunday of November or first of December	Christian New Year
(appropriate date)	Muslim New Year

Comment   On 1 January we go round saying 'Happy New Year'. A new calendar year begins. The world's religions, however, have their own New Year days.

READER A   The Zoroastrian New Year begins on 27 August. It is called Shanenshai. Listen now to a hymn of praise sung at that time.

READER B   Wise Lord, Lord of great thoughts:
Judge my life.
Give me the success I deserve
In the two kinds of life I lead:
First in the things that I do,
And in the things that happen to me.
And secondly, in the thoughts that I think,
And in the peace of my mind.
In both of these, please
Guide and help me,
And make me happy for ever.

READER A   The Jewish New Year begins about 13/14 September (changing every year) and is called Rosh Hashanah.

READER C   During the service in the synagogue that morning the ram's horn is blown, to proclaim God as king of the Universe. This day celebrates God's creation of the Universe. Ten days of penitence begins.

READER A   The Hindu New Year begins on 11 November, or rather at a day fixed by tradition in October–November. The festival is called Diwali.

READER D   This is the Indian New Year festival of lights when lamps are ceremonially lit, house fronts are illuminated and gifts exchanged. Lakshmi, the goddess of prosperity is believed to visit the homes lit by many lamps.

READER A   The Christian New Year begins on the first Sunday of Advent, which is either the last Sunday in November or the first in December.

READER E   On the first day of Advent, the Advent wreath and calendar begin. If a wreath is being used the first of four candles is lit or in homes that have the Advent calendar the first 'door' is opened. Both are step-by-step preparations for the great festival of Christ's birth.

READER A   The Muslim New Year changes from year to year.

READER F   The prophet Muhammad moved from Mecca to Medina in the year AD 622. There he organised his followers into a religious movement. The Muslim New Year begins with a celebration of the Prophet's action.

                (Five pupils still hold the New Year dates to view)

Comment   Different world religions begin their religious new year at different points in our year. *(Pupils turn placards to show name of world faith – then leave together.)* Wish your Jewish friends 'Happy New Year' in September, your Hindu friends 'Happy New Year' in November, your Christian friends in December, your Muslim friends whenever their New Year falls, and together let us wish each other a Happy New Calendar year on 1 January.

The Family

F46   The Family

Role-play   (*Two members of staff and one pupil, or three pupils, are needed.*) *Mother and father are sitting in armchairs (or simulated armchairs) watching TV – father reading newspaper at same time – mother knitting.*

FATHER   Look at that time! It's not good enough!

MOTHER   Well, it's only the second time – and he is 13 now.

FATHER   Yes – the second time this week!
(*Enter son or daughter*)

FATHER   Where do you think you've been?

BOY   (*placidly*) Out with my friends.

FATHER   Do you know what time it is? What do you think this place is – a hotel?

BOY   It's only just 10 o'clock, Dad.

FATHER   But I told you to be in at half past nine!

BOY   I said I might be a bit later – my friends don't have to be in until 10.

FATHER   I don't care what your friends do – you can't go out at all next week!

BOY   That's not fair. Mum, I was only a few minutes late.

MOTHER   Would you like a hot drink?

BOY   (*goes out slamming the door*) No, I'm going to bed.

Comment   A scene which, I'm sure, many of you are familiar with. A famous Roman writer named Pliny once said 'Home is where the heart is.' It's not that our hearts are not in our homes – we do love our family – but we feel that we

Reading

need to stand on our own two feet. We need to develop independence. Somehow we have got to balance love for our family and respect for our parents with a growing sense of responsibility for ourselves. Most people only learn to appreciate home and family properly when they become more mature. The following is taken from an interview with Roy Castle, the TV celebrity.

I realise that meeting and marrying Fiona was just the best thing that could have happened to me. For, quite apart from having given me four beautiful children, she gives me emotional security. And believe me, for a guy whose job it is to make people laugh, that's very important. Because security is the one thing most comedians find scarce.

You never know from one minute to the next whether you're going to be loved or hated, cheered or booed. And that's enough to turn the sanest guy neurotic.

Fiona and the kids make me feel that, whatever the future holds for me, I'll always be wanted and loved.

I was talking to an entertainer recently who told me he had made a conscious decision to concentrate on becoming a super-star at the expense of his family. For years he sought the limelight and the big time, and hardly spent any time at home. Finally, when he got home his two daughters were well into their teens. The bloke turned round to me and with deep regret in his voice admitted that the girls were total strangers to him.

And I thought to myself – what a waste. For no matter what you say, fame and fortune count for nothing compared to your own flesh and blood. What I've got is far more important than power.

And it's peace of mind. The one commodity in life you can't ever over-estimate.

Prayer

Heavenly Father you love and care for us as members of your family. Our parents love and care for us. Please help us when we disagree with our parents' point of view – when we think they are being unreasonable.

Help us to try to see their point of view and realise that they want to protect us from danger. May we grow to true maturity and personal responsibility but without hurt and damage to others. We ask this through Christ your Son. Amen.

Hymn   'God is love', CH 97, FP 43, HON 87, NL 132, NO 34, PL 276.

F47   Immigrants

Opening record 'Black and White', Greyhound, Trojan TR 7820 (*also by* The Spinners).

Comment   Over the centuries hundreds of thousands of people have come into the British Isles to settle down and make their home here.

READER A   The Vikings came as raiding parties in their long boats; they stole and murdered but eventually many settled and made this their home.

READER B   The Normans invaded and brought with them their French ways and language. The Saxon English resented them.

READER C   We had kings and queens of German blood who brought their people and customs with them.

READER D   Over the centuries Jewish traders and merchants came and settled; especially when they were expelled from their own native countries such as Russia and Germany.

READER E   The Irish came looking for work or driven out of their island by famine and oppressive landlords.

READER F   The British Empire spread and the Commonwealth. The Union Jack was the flag of the Colonies: English was their language and Victoria was their queen. From the Colonies and the Commonwealth they came to see their motherland and many made it their home.

Comment   The modern inhabitants of this country have originally come from many lands.

READER A   In my classroom there's all nations from all over the world, some from Jamaica, some from Hong Kong. I don't care, they're all friends to me. From the hot countries to the cold countries and from black to white, we're all friends in our classroom. Our class can prove to all prejudiced people all over the world that people from different nations can live together. My background is a cold place called Britain. It is cold in the winter and quiet in the summer, but not hot like in the other countries of America, India, Africa. The only difference between our countries is colour and language, and that's nothing really, we are all human and we can all show friendship and love for each other, and not war and hate between our colours.

Tommy Robertson

Scripture reading   Your trust in God your Father has made you members of his Family; Jesus has made this possible. For when you were baptised and became friends of Jesus, you began, with his help, to live in his way – as he lived in his Father's Way.

Living in God's Way means that you can't talk about one another as being 'white' or 'coloured', 'working-class' or 'upper-class', 'men' or 'women' – as though that were the only thing about them that matters. The most important thing is that as Christians you are one company of friends.

Galatians 3:26–29

Song   'The family of man', NL 113, NO 10, *or* 'When I needed a neighbour', CH 353, FH I 41, NL 123, NO 15, PL 298.

F48   Refugees

Opening record 'By the rivers of Babylon', Boney M, Atlantic K 11120.

Comment   That song is based upon a song or psalm that the Jews composed while in exile – like refugees – in a foreign land. What are refugees?

READER A   Because we never see refugees in our country we can easily not realise how many hundreds of thousands there are in different countries around the world. In time of war, thousands become refugees; in time of political unrest, thousands leave their home and try to find peace and security elsewhere; they become refugees. Every time you hear of fighting and war on the TV news there will be hundreds of people trying to get away from the troubled areas. Often they cannot get back to their homes – they become refugees.

Comment   Organisations like the Red Cross, the United Nations and Christian Aid try to help refugees. They need . . .

PUPIL 1   Food – because their crops are destroyed by bombing, tanks and all the mess-up of war.

PUPIL 2   Shelter – their homes are left behind and often destroyed or used for military purposes.

PUPIL 3   Medical care – travel and hardship affect especially the very young and the very old.

PUPIL 4   Loving care – for God said, 'Love your neighbour.'

READER B   If a stranger lives with you in your land, do not molest him. You must count him one of your own countrymen and love him as yourself – for you were once strangers yourself in Egypt.

Leviticus 19:33

Comment   Not only the Jewish people but Jesus himself was once a refugee.

READER C   After the Wise Men had left, the angel of the Lord appeared to Joseph in a dream and said, 'Get up, take the child and his mother with you, and escape into Egypt and stay there until I tell you, because Herod intends to search for the child and do away with him. So Joseph got up and, taking the child and his mother with him, left that night for Egypt.

Matthew 2:13–15

Comment   There's a song called 'No turning back'. Let us use the words in a response litany. After each verse please answer:

It's a long, long road,
No time to pack
Keep travelling on
No turning back.

READER A   Remember the people of Israel
Tramping the desert sands;
Hungry and anxious and weary,
Looking for the Promised Land:

ALL   It's a long, long road . . .

Herod's soldiers came hunting
A king that was to be,
But Mary and Joseph took Jesus
To Egypt as a refugee.

ALL   It's a long, long road . . .

Foxes have holes to hole up in:
Birds can fly home to bed,
But the Son of Mary (said Jesus)
Has nowhere to lay his head,

ALL   It's a long, long road . . .

Today there are families wandering
Parents and children too
No food, no clothes, no schooling,
And they've got no work to do.

ALL   It's a long, long road . . .

All they want is somewhere
That's free from fear and pain,
And a chance so they are able
To live in peace again.

ALL   It's a long, long road . . .

Comment   Let us pray the prayer of St Francis (*see* Alternative Assembly 1: *or sing the song version* 'Make me a channel', CH 189, FH I 35, FP 108, HON 167, SLW 97).

F49 Gypsies

Comment

Comments from a local paper: 'Pity the people of Dunton Green, on whom the gypsies have descended with their attendant piles of rubbish . . . it is difficult to stimulate the milk of human kindness towards gypsies in some of the desecrated areas with which we are all familiar. The sight of a roadside encampment is always a shock to the senses – no matter how often one sees it.'

Role-play

Village shop: woman serving from behind the counter, two villagers in shop, one being served, the other waiting. In walks a gypsy (could be man or woman). Behind the counter there is a sign which says, 'NO GYPSIES SERVED'. Talking in the shop stops. Shopkeeper looks at the gypsy then points, without a word, to the sign. Gypsy ignores her action. Customer at the counter turns and says 'Can't you read?' Gypsy says, 'Yes, but I only wanted a bag of sugar.' There follows an ad lib scene in which the gypsy argues that he (she) is human like anyone else – his money carries the same value, etc. The second customer accuses the shop-keeper of being 'a little unfair'. Scene finishes after a few minutes, once essential points have been made, with the shopkeeper saying, 'I'm calling the police' and the gypsy walking out of the shop.

READER A

The only possible solution to this most difficult problem is the establishment of properly planned and supervised sites for 'travelling families' as they are more generally known now.

READER B

It is estimated that there are over 7,000 travelling families in England and Wales. Since 1970, when the government passed the Caravan Site Act in Parliament, only 160 sites have been established. That means that two out of three gypsy families have no pitch or an official site. £30 million would have to be found to settle them. So far the money has not been found!

Prayer

Please reply to each invocation:
'Happy are the poor in spirit;
theirs is the kingdom of heaven.'

LEADER	We pray for those who feel unwanted in our community – especially the 7,000 travelling families.
ALL	Happy are the poor in spirit; theirs is the kingdom of heaven.
LEADER	We pray for those in our community who cannot read and write properly – especially for those who are among the travelling families.
ALL	Happy are the poor in spirit; theirs is the kingdom of heaven.
LEADER	We pray for those who are always being 'moved on' from one place to another – especially the travelling families.
ALL	Happy are the poor in spirit; theirs is the kingdom of heaven.
LEADER	We pray for those who close their hearts to those in need and develop prejudice – especially against the travelling families.
ALL	Happy are the poor in spirit; theirs is the kingdom of heaven.
LEADER	We pray for our government and those who can improve the lot of the 7,000 travelling families.
ALL	Happy are the poor in spirit; theirs is the kingdom of heaven.

F50   The Hungry

Comment	*(Four pupils sit on stage, or assembly area, in a line, facing the rest; between the third and fourth pupil there is a space.)* There is great hunger in the world. For every one of us that has enough to eat *(the fourth pupil stands up)* there are three who go to bed hungry every night *(the remaining three stand up)*.
FOURTH PUPIL	*(speaking to the assembled gathering)* We've got a colour TV set and a new TV game to go with it.
THIRD PUPIL	My family lives on the pavement in the city of Calcutta and we're lucky if we get one meal a day.

FOURTH PUPIL	My Dad has just got a new car. It can do 110 miles an hour.
SECOND PUPIL	My family live in a hut of corrugated iron in Peru and when we're lucky we get one meal a day.
FOURTH PUPIL	On our holidays we took our caravan to the seaside. We've also got a speed-boat.
FIRST PUPIL	My Dad had to leave us to find work in Hong Kong. Sometimes my brothers and sisters find enough food for us to get one meal a day.
Comment	There's no doubt about it, everyone in this room (*or* hall) is rich compared with most of the world.

Reading

VOICE 1	Whose are the voices crying, crying? Whose are the pitiful pleas we hear? Whose is the sorrow that finds tongue in weeping? Whose hopelessness speaks with despair?
VOICE 2	Ours are the voices crying, crying; Ours are the pitiful pleas you hear. We are the people you hear at our weeping. Ours is the empty cry of despair.
VOICE 1	Whose are the faces so drawn with suffering? Whose are the bodies no more than bones? Whose are the eyes that are hopeless and lifeless? Whose are the graves with nameless stones?
VOICE 2	Ours are the faces gaunt with starvation. Ours are the wasted dying frames. Ours are the hungry eyes of the hopeless. Ours are the graves with no names.
VOICE 1	Why do I hear your cries of starvation? Why show me hunger I don't wish to see? Why are your skeleton fingers still reaching Endlessly, endlessly out to me?
VOICE 2	Have we been changed so much by our suffering? In our extremity aren't we the same? Brother to brother, we reach out our hands to you. Flesh of one flesh are we, name of one name.

VOICE 1	What can I do for you, brother, my brother? How can I help? I am too far away. Leave it to God, hungry brother, my brother. Go down on your thin starving knees, and pray.
VOICE 2	We have prayed, distant brother, with fierce desperation.
VOICE 1	Has God in His Mercy shown what you must do?
VOICE 2	He has, brother, answered our earnest entreaties, He has answered our prayers and his answer is YOU.

Anon., from Redvers Brandling, Assembly

Comment Do you remember the words of Jesus? When he said that whatever we do to another person we do to him. So if we ignore the hungry we ignore Christ – but if we help them, we help him.

Scripture reading

I was hungry and you gave me food;
I was thirsty and you gave me drink;
I was a foreigner and you took me home with you;
I was in rags and you gave me clothes;
I fell ill and you looked after me;
I was in prison and you came to see me.
Believe me –
when you helped the least of my brothers,
you helped me.

I was hungry and you gave me no food;
I was thirsty and you gave me no drink;
I was a foreigner and you didn't take me home with you;
I was in rags and you gave me no clothes;
I fell ill and you didn't look after me;
I was in prison and you never came to see me.
Believe me –
When you didn't help the least of my brothers,
you didn't help me.

Alan T. Dale, New World

Hymn 'Whatsoever you do', CH 352, FH I 71, FP 180, HON 298, *or* 'When I needed a neighbour', CH 353, FH I 41, NL 123, NO 13, PL 298.

General Themes

G51   Thanksgiving

Opening record   'Thank you for the music', Abba, from *Abba's Greatest Hits*, vol. 2 *(fade after 1 min. 15 sec.)*.

Reading   In 1939, Sgt-Major Robert McCormack saved the life of his commanding officer, Major Harry Parkin, on the battlefield in France during the British withdrawal to Dunkirk. He has just received his 40th annual letter of thanks from Harry Parkin, now a retired estate agent of Richmond, Yorkshire. 'Dear Bob', Parkin wrote, 'I want to thank you for the 40 years of life which ordinarily I would not have had, were it not for you. You know I'm grateful to you.'

Comment   It's not very likely that most of us will ever have the opportunity of saving another person's life – and I hope none of you are ever in the situation where you are in need of rescue. However, our thanks are due to God for our very existence, not to mention all those little things which make life happy – music, football, TV, for example.

Record   *(As background to the following)* 'Thank you for the music', Abba.

READER A   Almighty God, we want to thank you for our lives and everything that makes them happy.

READER B   Thank you for the TV and our favourite programmes – may we use TV well.

READER C   Thank you for pop music and for . . . . and . . . . *(add current favourite pop groups)* – may we learn to make music of our own, to give joy to others.

READER D   Thank you for Radio One *(or Capital Radio or other local station)* – may we never use it to annoy other people who do not share our tastes.

READER E   Thank you for the game of football that gives pleasure to so many people, especially 'thank you' for helping our favourite teams to do well – may we always respect other people both when we watch and play football.

READER F   Thank you for our homes, families, school, teachers and fellow pupils – may we always show love and respect to those around us.

Poster   (PTP 4 'Thank you Father for making me, Me' *if available can be shown at this point*).

Comment   We are as we are. We cannot change our height, our looks, our gifts and talents, our brothers and sisters – or our parents or teachers. Accepting ourselves as we are – with all that we have or do not have – and being grateful for it, that is an important key to happiness.

Hymn   'Thank you', CH 298, FH I 95, HON 257, PL 275 *or* 'Now thank we all our God', AM 379, CH 211, HON 180, NL 55, NO 33, PL 93.

G52   Freedom

Opening record 'I'm free', Roger Daltry, Ode ODS 66302 (*fade for reading*).

Comment   This was the headline in the *Daily Mail* on 17 September 1979: 'Families escape to West by balloon! UP, UP AND AWAY TO FREEDOM'.

Reading 1   Two young families yesterday brought off the most fantastic defection of all – over the East–West German border at 1,500ft in a home-made hot-air balloon.

Four adults and four children, the youngest only two years old, made a 30 minute flight to freedom clinging to a wooden platform about 4½ft square.

Above them was the balloon envelope, 137ft high, and 114ft across stitched together by the two wives from nylon sheets and curtains. The platform had a single safety precaution, a clothes rope wound round four corner posts. The children were at the corners, the adults hung on to a flimsy cage in the middle which contained four large cylinders of butane gas to power crude hot air burners. This was the extraordinary craft that rose into the night sky at 2.40 am from a remote field outside the East German village of Poessnek, in the province of Thuringia. Six miles to the south lay the border, Bavaria – and freedom. It had taken a nail-biting hour to inflate the balloon.

It was a clear, starlit night and the wind was right. But it was bitterly cold and they were terrified.

At one awful moment, during the flight, a search-light presumably manned by Communist border guards, actually caught the balloon. The escapers waited for the shooting to start – but, inexplicably, nothing happened.

The pilot and the man who designed the balloon, was 37-year-old aircraft mechanic Hans-Peter Strelzik. His friend Gunther Wetzel helped him to build it while the wives sewed. They bought the material bit by bit in different places so as not to attract attention and hid it in the cellar.

They did it, Strelzik said, 'because it was no longer possible for us to lie to our children and put up with the political conditions.'

Yesterday's flight ended abruptly and dangerously, when the gas ran out and the balloon came down too fast. They survived the bump with minor bruises – but they did not know how far they had come. They thought they must be over the border because they saw 'a modern farm machine unlike anything we have', said Strelzik.

The two men hid in a barn and wondered. Then they saw a patrol car, a man in uniform. Strelzik and Wetzel had to chance it. They approached and asked 'Are we in the West?'

The answer told them they had made it. They were two miles over the border.

Daily Mail

Comment   It's amazing what people will endure to find freedom. It's a natural drive – to be free. But what does it mean?

VOICE A   Freedom for me means staying out as long as *I* like at night.

VOICE B   Freedom for me means doing what *I* like – at home and at school.

VOICE C   Freedom for me means wearing what *I* like and when *I* like.

VOICE D   Freedom for me means no rules and regulations – no police, no teachers telling you what to do.

Comment   But is that real freedom? Listen carefully to what some famous wise men have said about real freedom.

READER A   Gandhi said, 'Freedom is not worth having if it does not include the freedom to make mistakes.'

READER B   Charles Kingsley said, 'There are two freedoms – the false, where a man is free to do what he likes; the true, where a man is free to do what he ought.'

READER C   Field Marshal Lord Montgomery said 'True freedom is freedom to do what we ought to do. It is not freedom to do as we like.'

Comment   So real freedom does not keep saying 'I want' 'I must have.' Freedom does not come from disrespecting others – from pushing yourself forward with no concern for your duty to others, especially the needy and the weak.

READER   Christ came to make men free
                 Free from their isolation and their fear.
                 He came –
                 Homeless – and so at home among all;
                 In poverty – and so the guest of all;
                 In weakness – and so at the mercy of all;
                 Common – and so approachable by all;
                 A man with time for all,
                 A man for others.

                                                      Jim Bates

Prayer   Almighty Father you made men to be free. Help all those who seek freedom from tyranny of any kind. Help us to understand the true nature of freedom so that we may not be wrapt in the tyranny of our own self-love. May we learn to imitate the most free of all men – your Son Jesus Christ who gave himself for others. We ask this through the same Christ our Lord. Amen.

G53   Hope

Opening record 'Chiquitita', Abba, from *Abba's Greatest Hits*, vol. 2 (*fade after 2 min. 15 sec.*).

Comment The record says 'Sing a new song – the sun is still shining above you.' That is what hope is: continuing to believe that the sun is above the clouds on a cloudy day, ready to break through.

Reading News headline in *Sunday Mirror*, 19 August 1979, 'Chief Constable talks of "slender hope".'

On Saturday, 19 August, at about 3.30 pm, pretty Genette Tate, aged 13, disappeared mysteriously without trace. She was riding her bicycle down a narrow lane in Aylesbeare, when she disappeared, leaving her bicycle in the road and no clues. Over £1 million has been spent on the search for her, 7,000 local people helped in the search, tens of thousands of people were interviewed and £35,000 offered in reward money if she should be found or returned to her parents, but the police search has produced nothing – not one shred of evidence. Some people have suggested that she may have been taken away in an UFO, and while it cannot be completely ruled out, there is no evidence to support the theory.

Chief Constable John Alderson believes she is dead, murdered by a psychopathic killer, but he cannot rule out the slender hope that she is still alive. Her parents cling to that hope.

Comment We say 'While there's life there's hope.' No matter how bad things are we should always hope and of course, pray.

Reading   To hope means to be ready
at every moment
for that which is not yet born,
and yet not become desperate
if there is no birth in our lifetime.
There is no sense in hoping
for that which already exists
or for that which cannot be.
Those whose hope is weak
settle down for comfort or for violence;
those whose hope is strong
see and cherish all signs of new life
and are ready every moment
to help the birth
of that which is ready to be born.

Erich Fromm

Poster   Argus 42651: 'When the outlook is bad try looking up'.
Show this poster (or PT 45), *if available, and play part
of the opening record again.*

Prayer   Lord, it's just when we most need the light of your love
in our lives that we least feel like asking for it. When
things go wrong and life seems dismal and grey and
hardly worth living, be with us Lord to support and
strengthen us. Help us never to forget that your Son,
the light of the world, is always smiling upon us. Ready
to lift us up and fill our lives again with joy. Please hear
our prayer through the same Christ our Lord. Amen.

G54   Charity

Comment   Do you know the old saying 'Red sky at night,
shepherd's delight; red sky in the morning, shepherd's
warning'? That's a very old weather saying. Even the
Jews of the time of Jesus had a similar version of it.

Reading   The Pharisees and the Sadducees came, and to test him
they asked if he would show them a sign from heaven.
He replied. 'In the evening you say, "It will be fine;

there is a red sky", and in the morning "Stormy weather today; the sky is red and overcast." You know how to read the face of the sky, but you cannot read the signs of the times.'

Matthew 16:1–3

Comment   Naomi James was a young woman who on 9 September 1977 set out from Dartmouth to sail round the world on her own. She had never sailed alone before and she not only succeeded, but made sailing history by doing it in record time. However, it was a very hard and difficult voyage.

Reading   Wedged into a corner of the cockpit, muffled against the cold by thick oilskins, I watched intently as the light faded slowly from the sky. Lines of black rain squalls welled up over the horizon and passed low overhead, every now and then hitting *Crusader* with a savage blast of wind and rain.

Somewhere behind that wall of cloud the sun was setting, and I searched the sky anxiously for a hint of colour – red or even the faintest touch of pink – which would tell me there wasn't going to be a storm tomorrow.

Before the last storm the weather had looked the same as this but the sky had been copper, an ominous greenish-yellow colour, which made my heart sink.

Every night since then I had watched, staying on deck till my hands and face froze, knowing that *Crusader* probably couldn't stand another storm with her damaged mast, held up by my makeshift rigging.

I still had to sail over a thousand miles to reach Cape Horn. The very thought of it sent a shiver down my spine. Another two weeks or more before I could reach the safety of the Falkland Islands . . . if ever.

I no longer thought of getting there but simply of getting through each day as it came. More and more often I thought what am I doing here? What on earth possessed me to come down to the lumpy, unfriendly and empty Southern Ocean?

Comment   Courageous Naomi had learned to read the natural weather signs – the red sky. Did you realise that we give out signals or signs to other people all day long, of the sort of people we are. Jesus said 'by their fruits you will know them' – that is, kind unselfish people can be recognised by their kind courteous acts – selfish, mean people do selfish mean things.

Scripture
reading
We are members of God's family, and I ask you to remember two things: keep God's kindness always in your minds, and give yourselves heart and soul to him – your energy, your heart and your mind. You belong to God, and it is service like this that makes God glad.

Don't try to do 'what everybody else does'; let God keep your mind alive and ready to think new thoughts, and you'll be a very different person from what you were. In this way you will be able to find out what God wants you to be and to do – what is worth-while and right and grown-up.

Romans 12:1–5 (*New World*)

Comment
'See how these Christians love one another' said the pagans of Ancient Rome. They were impressed when they saw the signs. If you want to be thought well of, you too must show signs of caring and concern for others.

Hymn
'Bind us together, Lord', FH IV 21, HON 33, *or* 'Love is his word', CH 185, FH I 66, FP 107, HON 166, PL 75.

G55   Peace

Role-play
Persons required for roles of mother, father, 'child' and three voices. The 'family' are sitting watching TV (side view of a cardboard box will do!).

VOICE 1
(from TV set) The news tonight is of the invasion of Cyprus by Turkey. Airborne troops fell from the sky as landing barges hit the beaches of the northern coastline . . .

MOTHER
Turn it over, dear, we don't want to hear that dismal news of people suffering – war, war, war *(child gets up and switches programme over)*.

VOICE 2	This evening's BBC 2 *Man Alive* programme is on Northern Ireland. Since January a record number of soldiers and civilians have been killed and injured. *Man Alive* looks at . . .
FATHER	See what's on ITV? *(child gets up again and switches the programme over).*
VOICE 3	*(preceded by a hammering noise)* It is a great tragedy when a young mother has to barricade herself in her home against a violent drunken husband. In our stressful society wife-battering seems to be on the increase . . . *(without a word child gets to his feet and turns the TV off).*
CHILD	Why is life so violent, Dad? Is there no peace anywhere?
FATHER	Well at least there's peace in our home, isn't there?
Comment	'Why is life so violent?' What a difficult question! At least the father was right in pointing out that peace has always got to begin with us. Whether it is violence on the grand scale – war; or the smaller, but just as terrifying terrorist activities in our own country – or violence in a family. Peace must begin with us.
Poster	PTP 22, 'Peace starts with a smile' *(or* PT 41) *or* Argus 42715-A 'Let there be peace on earth and let it begin with me.'
Comment	*(showing first poster)* As Mother Teresa says here, 'Peace begins with a smile.' But a genuine smile means that you have peace inside yourself.
Reading	Peace is not won By man's eternal strife, Peace is the power of God In human life. It dwells with joy and love, Is manifest in grace; The star above His crib, The light that is His face.

Anon.

Prayer   Give us, O God, the vision which can see thy love in
              the world in spite of human failure. Give us the faith,
              the trust, the goodness in spite of our ignorance and
              weakness. Give us the knowledge that we may continue
              to pray with understanding hearts, and show us what
              each one of us can do to set forth the coming of the day
              of universal peace.

              *If the following hymn is not going to be sung, the Prayer of
              St Francis (see Alternative Assembly 1) could well be used.*

Song   'Make me a channel of your peace', CH 189, FH I 35, FP
              108, HON 167, SLW 97.

G56   Unsolved Mysteries

Comment   Do you believe in ghosts? Poltergeists? UFOs? Here is
              the first of two recent newspaper reports.

Reading 1   At Broadhaven School, 14 children aged between 10
              and 11 told their headmaster they had seen a UFO land
              200 yards from where they were playing. He separated
              them and told them to draw what they saw. Their
              drawings matched. So did their reports.
                 Headmaster Richard Llewelin said: 'Children of that
              age aren't capable of maintaining such an elaborate
              hoax.' It is an area bristling with defence establish-
              ments, some highly secret. The RAF confirmed a flood
              of reports, and said the sightings did not match their
              operations.
                                          The Sun, 22 August 1979

Comment   Each year there are thousands of sightings of strange
              shapes up above us. Around 2,000 people, throughout
              the world, have claimed to have actually met UFO
              crews – humanoids. Is it all deception? A hoax? Do
              other intelligent beings visit our planet? Gordon
              Cooper, US astronaut says this:

Reading 2   The American Space Agency and government know
              that intelligent beings from other planets visit our

world. They have an enormous amount of evidence but have kept quiet.

Comment   UFOs are only part of the mysterious unseen world about us. What do you make of this report in the *Daily Mail*, 11 September 1979?

Reading 3   On the evening of 6 August 1979, Madame Bourdat, of the little French village of Seron, was herding her few cows past an abandoned farmhouse, when she noticed smoke billowing out of a downstairs room. She rushed to her neighbours, the Lahore family, who own the disused building and together they put the fire out. Within two hours, two more mysterious fires broke out, this time in the Lahores' modern farmhouse. In the following few weeks 90 fires broke out, no-one, yet, has succeeded in finding an explanation. Despite the efforts of mediums, psychologists, priests, exorcists and police and fire experts from Tarbes and Paris, no explanation or cause has yet come to light. Several witnesses have seen the fires begin. First there is a smell of smoke, then a charred spot appears which after a few moments bursts into flame. The burning object is rushed out of the house to be doused by one of the policemen on duty there. On one hair-raising day alone, 32 separate fires broke out in the house. At one time or another nearly every conceivable item in the house has been burned, even clothes while the Lahores were wearing them. No one on the spot, either in the Lahore family itself or from the constant stream of specialists and experts that have streamed through the house, has come up with an explanation. Police in Tarbes and Paris have had to admit that they can offer no help or guidance as to the cause of the strange happenings at the Lahore farmhouse.

Comment   That story seems to point to poltergeists, but who knows? Of course to believe in God is to believe in a spirit world, an unseen world. Many experts are seeking ways of exploring this unseen world in much the same way as the old explorers courageously discovered that the world, as was believed at the time, was not flat. Whatever the explanation of these mysteries one thing is certain, God is still creator of all and master of all. Let us have a healthy interest and open and enquiring minds but take care not to fill our minds with pointless rubbish.

Scripture reading

Fill our minds with everything that is true, everything that is noble, everything that is good and pure, everything that we love and honour, and everything that can be thought virtuous or worthy of praise.

Philippians 4:8

Comment

Our faith and trust at all times must be in Christ who is over all things.

Scripture reading

He is the image of the unseen God and the first born of all creation, for in him were created all things in heaven and on earth: everything visible and invisible, Thrones, Domination, Sovereignties, Powers – all things were created through him and for him. Before anything was created, he existed, and he holds all things in unity.

Colossians 1:15–17

Hymn

'O Lord my God', CH 227, FH II 27, FP 8, HON 202 *or* 'All the nations of the earth', CH 12, FH I 81, FP 62, HON 17.

G57   Loneliness

Comment

Many of you, I know, have pets. Do you think they miss you when you are away? When Naomi James, who sailed round the world on her own, lost her pet cat, she was very lonely.

Reading

On 28 October (day 50) I wrote in my log: 'Boris and I got a dowsing this morning. When we went on deck I hadn't bothered to put up my oilskin hood, and I took a full dollop of sea down my neck. Boris had been perched on the jib winch and he got it as well. He looked shocked and shook himself, but he didn't remove himself below as I thought he would. He looks so funny when he gallops along the heeling deck with his ears flat and his fur fluffed up, but I'm sure he doesn't mind getting wet.'

The next morning, at eight o'clock, Boris went over the side.

After a senseless search of two and a half hours, I sat down at the chart table and forced myself to write the following:

'Boris has gone. I feel numb and unable to think straight, but I'm going to write this down so that I can begin to accept that it has happened and there's nothing more I can do. Nothing. Shortly after breakfast, I was on the foredeck getting the ghoster ready to hoist when I saw him doing his daredevil act of walking on the toe rail around the boat's edge. I reached out to pull him back, but he came in voluntarily; then I must have turned away. A few minutes later, out of the corner of my eye, I saw him lurch – as he had several times before – but this time he went over and I rushed to the stern to disconnect the self-steering gear and put the wheel hard over.

'Then I dashed to the mast to let go the mainsail and stay-sail halyards. I could see him in the wake about 50 yards away and *Crusader* was slowly turning around towards him. But then I had to go below to start the engine and although it took only a matter of seconds, when I got back to the wheel he had disappeared.

'When I was past the place where I'd seen him last, I cut the engine, called and listened. There was nothing to be seen or heard. I called and called like a fool and steered the boat round in circles, but it was no use and eventually I told myself to stop.

'It was so calm and there were barely more than a few ripples on the surface, but Boris was nowhere to be seen.'

Comment   Naomi was really cut off from any living contact, really alone. We often think of old people as being lonely – and many are – but anyone of any age can be lonely. There are lonely people in this school – in your class.

Reading

'Dear Daddy' – in her best handwriting 11-year-old Jane wrote a letter to her make-believe father every week. She addressed the envelope to herself, and every week without fail she wrote back 'Dear Jane'. For this shy youngster living in a local authority home two postage stamps and a dream father were the only cure she had available for an affliction that is so pathetically easy to diagnose – loneliness. At this moment there are four million desperately lonely people in this country. Before someone like young Jane grows into a lonely Mrs X I know who rings up the telephone speaking clock for company, why don't we act?

Daily Express

Poster

PTP 9, *or* Argus 42456-A.

Comment

Yes, why don't we. People are often lonely because they are shy (*showing the poster*). If you feel lonely, note what this says, 'People are lonely because they build walls instead of bridges.' An effort must be made to reach out to others. Those of us who are not lonely should look out for those who are and help them to build bridges to other people. It is very important for all of us to remember that God is always with us, wherever we are or whatever we are doing.

Scripture reading

Make your home in me, as I make mine in you. As a branch cannot bear fruit all by itself, but must remain part of the vine, neither can you unless you remain in me.

John 15:4–7

You are my friends, if you do what I command you. I shall not call you servants any more, because a servant does not know his master's business; I call you friends, because I have made known to you everything I have learnt from my Father.

John 15:14

Prayer

Lord, I often feel the need of friendship; someone close to me, someone I can trust completely. I know you are always close to me and want to be my friend. The trouble is, Lord, I so easily forget how near at hand you are, and how willing you are to help. Please help me to remember your love and your closeness. Amen.

G58 Elderly People

Role-play/ ***reading***	*Two pupils (boy and girl preferably) required as Mr and Mrs Phillips (in early 80s), another as the local social worker. Three or four 'off-stage' voices needed. Old couple sitting at kitchen table having breakfast.*
MR PHILLIPS	*(reading a letter)* 'A car will take you to the station and you will be met at Great Yarmouth station by a taxi which will take you to the hotel.'
MRS PHILLIPS	I can't really believe it – our first holiday for ten years. And free too. I can't believe it.
MR PHILLIPS	*(laying down the letter and picking up a piece of toast)* That social worker was right. I never thought we would qualify for a free holiday – I suppose being over 80 helps!
	(There's the sound of smashing glass and half a house-brick lands on the table, smashing and scattering the table things. Mrs Phillips screams and slumps in her chair. Mr Phillips is stunned for a moment then moves to the shattered window. Laughing voices are heard and someone shouts, 'Go to work on a brick.' Mr Phillips returns to console Mrs Phillips who sits bolt upright, trembling and crying.)
MR PHILLIPS	Come and lay down, dear, then I'll go next door and phone the police again.
MRS PHILLIPS	You know you're wasting your time. *(Door bell rings.)*
MR PHILLIPS	*(picking up a walking stick)* If it's those kids from that Comprehensive again I'll show them what for.
	(Mr Phillips disappears and returns with the social worker, who is speaking.)
SOCIAL WORKER	Have you had the letter yet about your free holiday? *(Seeing the weeping old lady)* Why, Mrs Phillips, what's the matter? *(Then, seeing the damage everywhere)* What's happened? Who did it? Not the kids from the Comprehensive again!
MR PHILLIPS	Yes, the new glass had only been in two days. That's it, we can't go.

SOCIAL WORKER	What do you mean – you can't go?
MR PHILLIPS	We can't go away on holiday and leave our home to be smashed into again and again by those thugs. It's the parents' fault. The police say that the headmaster can't trace who's doing it.
MRS PHILLIPS	*(now calmed)* That's the second time in a week. We can't go on holiday and leave our home to that.
SOCIAL WORKER	We could board up the window. You *must* take this free holiday.
MR PHILLIPS	No, that's final. We cannot go and leave our home. I fought in the 14–18 war for this country and all my friends were killed; I was an air-raid warden in the last war. We never thought we were saving this country to become fit only for young thugs.
Comment	If we could interview the three pupils that did such a cowardly and sickening thing they would tell us that they did it for 'kicks', 'for a laugh'. They'd say that old people are 'finished' anyway. Remember these facts:
READER A	Fact number one – your grandparents are old people.
READER B	Fact number two – your parents will, in a few years time, be old people.
READER C	Fact number three – you will one day be an old person.
READER D	Fact number four – we are all equal in God's sight, whatever our age and each one of us will die.
Comment	Christ did not tell us to love the people we like or those of our own age group. He said:
READER A	'Love one another as I have loved you.'
	John 15:12
READER B	'What I command you is to love one another.'
	John 15:17
READER C	'Whatsoever you do to the least person you do to me.'
	Matthew 24:40

Hymn	'Whatsoever you do', CH 352, FH I 71, FP 180, HON 298 *or* 'When I needed a neighbour', CH 353, FH I 41, NL 123, NO 13, PL 298.

G59   Perseverance

Opening record	'Money, money, money', Abba, Epic 4713 *(fade after 30 sec.)*.
Comment	Have you ever really looked at a £1 note? Can anyone tell me whose picture appears on the back of the note? Isaac Newton's. What was he famous for? Yes, everyone knows that he was the man who discovered and developed the laws of gravity. Do you know this story of Sir Isaac?
Reading	Sir Isaac Newton was a famous scientist who owned a dog called Diamond. Diamond did him a very bad turn. Newton had taken eight whole years to write a very important book. One morning he came into his room and found that Diamond had knocked over a candle and the candle had set fire to the book on his desk. Think what that meant; eight whole years of work burnt up, but he could not be angry with a dog that did not know what it was doing. Newton said, 'Diamond, little do you know the labour and trouble to which you have put your master.' Then he did not look upon that great work as lost for ever as most people would have done. He sat down at his desk to start all over again.

M. Nassan

Comment	That's called 'perseverance'. The ability to stick at a thing until it's finished. Often we need help to persevere. Another Newton – John Newton – composed a famous hymn about the help necessary to stick at something, to persevere – we call it grace.
Hymn	'Amazing Grace', CH 19, FH I 36, FP 73, HON 20, SLW 5.

Litany prayer   Each time I say 'Give us the grace, O Lord', please answer 'that we may persevere'.

A wise man once said 'every noble work is at first impossible'. May we never give up on a good idea. Give us the grace, O Lord.

ALL   That we may persevere.

It is hard to keep trying to be good and kind. May we never give up trying to be better persons. Give us the grace, O Lord.

ALL   That we may persevere.

Obedience to parents, teachers, rules and regulations is particularly difficult. May we never give up trying. Give us the grace, O Lord.

ALL   That we may persevere.

When we see so much evil in the world it is tempting to give up believing in God. May we hold on to our faith and give us the grace, O Lord.

ALL   That we may persevere.

Schoolwork is sometimes boring and a hard slog. May we never give in to laziness and complacency. Give us the grace, O Lord.

ALL   That we may persevere.

Comment   May the grace of our Lord Jesus Christ and the love of God and the fellowship of the Holy Spirit be with you all. Amen.

G60   Quiet – Time for Prayer

Opening record   'Halfway down the stairs', Muppets, Pye 7N 45698 *(fade after short introduction)*.

Comment   The Muppets are world famous. Their shows are shown on TV sets in 102 countries, and watched by 235 million viewers. Their fans think of them not as just loveable puppets but as real-life people with thoughts and feelings.

READER A   Everyone knows that Miss Piggy is in love with Kermit the frog. She dreams of marrying him!

READER B   Kermit seems to be the only sane muppet around. But when told this he said 'Me not crazy? But I hired the others!'

READER C   The Great Gonzo is really crazy. He accepts failure and looks on it as success.

READER D   Fozzie Bear's whole life is *The Muppet Show*. He gets to the theatre first and just sits on the door step. He is a sad and lonely figure.

Record   *Replay* 'Halfway down the stairs'.

Comment   This is sung by Kermit's nephew Robin and everyone has experienced the same feeling: the need to be alone. Lots of people have favourite spots where they go for a few moments or few hours of peace and quiet. Jesus too used to do this.

Scripture readings

READER A   When Jesus received the news of John the Baptist's death he withdrew by boat to a lonely place where they could be by themselves.
                                                          Matthew 14:13

READER B   After sending the crowds away Jesus went up into the hills by himself to pray.
                                                          Matthew 14:23

READER C   In the morning, long before dawn, Jesus got up and left the house, and went off to a lonely place and prayed there.
                                                          Mark 1:35

Poster   PT 16, 'Be still and know that I am God' (*or* PT 54).

Comment   If we are serious about being Christians then we too must give time to being quiet – when we can pray. This poster says 'Be still and know that I am God' – God cannot get through to us if we don't allow some time of quiet. It doesn't matter where. It could be half-way down the stairs or on a quiet walk or in a church.

Prayer

Lord, life is one long rush. Even when I sit down quietly I feel I ought to be doing something. Teach me how to be still and quiet. Help me to enjoy being with you in peace, help me to experience your presence. Please help me at all times to trust completely in you and your love for me. May your deep peace always fill me and those I love. Amen.

Song

'Peace, perfect peace', CH 257, FH I 2, FP 120, HON 220 *or* 'Peace is flowing like a river', CH 254, FH II 31, FP 221, HON 219, SLW 91.

ALTERNATIVE ASSEMBLIES

These Alternative Assemblies require little
or no preparation and are structured more formally
than the Prepared Assemblies of the previous section.
A Bible is required for the Alternative Assemblies.

1   Community

Hymn

'All people that on earth do dwell', AM 166, CH 10, HON 14, NL 44, PL 11.

Reading

In America in the 1860s, when covered wagons were heading west, the leaders always dreaded the fording of the River Platte. The current was so changeable in the broad, muddy stream that not even experienced scouts could tell where the pockets of quicksand and potholes lay. When an ox-team got stuck, the wagon was usually overturned, dumping family and possessions into the river. The difficulty was easily overcome. When a large number of wagons had arrived at the river, the oxen from all of them were hitched together in a long line to pull each of the families across in turn. Even though one team in the long line floundered there were always enough on sure footing to keep the wagon on the move.

Anon.

Comment

On our own we often feel lost; we feel the need of other people's help and support. Being of help and support to one another is the way God wants it to be.

Scripture reading

Acts 2:42–47 or *New World*, p.166.

Prayer

Almighty God, we pray thee to give thy blessing to this school community. Help all of us gathered here to work for a greater togetherness and harmony. May we care for one another and the health and well-being of every member of our community. We ask this through Jesus Christ our Lord. Amen.

Hymn

'Bind us together, Lord', FH IV 21, HON 33.

ALTERNATIVES

Reading   See assembly 2.

Hymn   'The family of man', NL 113, NO 10.
'We are gathering together', CH 341, FH II 79, FP 172, HON 293.
'We are one in the Spirit', CH 342, FH I 46, HON 294, PL 296.

Prayer   Lord, make me an instrument of thy peace;
Where there is hatred, let me sow love;
Where there is injury, pardon;
Where there is discord, union;
Where there is doubt, faith;
Where there is despair, hope;
Where there is darkness, light;
Where there is sadness, joy.

St Francis of Assisi

2   Need for One Another

Hymn   'Oh when the saints go marching in', CH 232, FH I 91, PL 82.

Comment   While that song can be heard on the football terraces on a Saturday afternoon, it is a famous traditional hymn. A hymn with a serious meaning. It reminds us that we cannot get to heaven on our own – we need other people.

Reading   No man is an island, entire of itself: every man is a piece of the continent, a part of the main; if a clod be washed away by the sea, Europe is the less, as well as if a promontory were, as well as if a manor of thy friends or of thine were. Any man's death diminishes me, because I am involved in mankind. And therefore never send to know for whom the bell tolls; it tolls for thee.

John Donne

Comment   That reading was from a famous English writer, John Donne. The important and famous words to remember were 'No man is an island' – we are not cut off from one another, like a tiny island way out in the Pacific Ocean. We need and depend on one another.

Scripture reading　Romans 12:3–13, or, preferably, *New World*, p.322.

Prayer

Break through, break through, Lord God,
Break through our meanness and narrow selfishness.
Make us care about our class-mates,
Make us concerned about the lonely in our school,
Make us realise the need we have for one another.

Open our eyes to our own selfishness, that we may learn that we need others as they need us.
Give us patience,
Give us reconciliation,
For your name's sake. Amen.

Hymn　'When I needed a neighbour', CH 353, FH I 41, NL 123, NO 13, PL 298.

ALTERNATIVES

Reading　See assembly 1.

Hymns

'Bind us together, Lord', FH IV 21, HON 33.
'The family of man', NL 113, NO 10.
'We are one in the Spirit', CH 342, FH I 46, HON 294, PL 296.

Prayers　See assembly 1 or 31.

3　Communication

Hymn　'Love is his word', CH 185, FH I 66, FP 107, HON 166, PL 75.

Reading 1

Words are the bridges we build
To reach each other.

Hands can talk, by touch they say
Many things in a clear distinct way.
They can wave, hold, shake, pat and point,

Soothe, slap, curl, take and anoint.
Eyes can talk. By look they tell
Many a thing that mouths hide well.

But to bring an idea from behind a face
Shaped to perfection and spun into space,
And held up to feast the whole human race
Alive in performance, still supple and true
This – only the written word can do.

Mary O'Neill

Comment   It is not only the written word, the spoken word is
powerful too. Jesus said, 'It is from the overflow of the
heart that the mouth speaks'. In other words the sort of
people we are will show up in what we say and how we
say it.

Reading 2   Never let a thought shrivel and die
For want of a way to say it,
For English is a wonderful game
And all of you can play it.
All that you do is match your words
To the brightest thoughts in your head
So that they come out clear and true
And handsomely groomed and fed –
For many of the loveliest things
Have never yet been said.
Words are the food and dress of thought,
They give it its body and swing,
And everyone's longing today to hear
Some fresh and beautiful thing.
But only words can free a thought
From its prison behind your eyes.
Maybe your mind is holding now
A marvellous new surprise!

Mary O'Neill

Prayer   O God, take control of me all through today,
Control my tongue,
So that I may speak
No angry word;
No cruel word;
No untrue word;

No ugly word.
Control my thoughts,
So that I may think
No impure thoughts;
No bitter, envious, or jealous thoughts;
No selfish thoughts.
Control my actions,
So that all through today
My work may be my best;
I may never be too busy to lend a hand to those who need it;
I may do nothing of which afterwards I would be ashamed.
All this I ask for Jesus's sake. Amen.

Hymn   'Make me a channel of your peace', CH 189, FH I 35, FP 108, HON 167, SLW 97.

ALTERNATIVES

Hymns   'God is love', CH 97, FP 43, HON 87, NL 132, NO 34, PL 276
'Let all that is within me', CH 167, FH I 15, FP 159, HON 148, SLW 20.
'Lord, I want to be a Christian', SLW 36.

Prayers   See assembly 44 or 21.

4   Truth

Hymn   'Mine eyes have seen the glory', CH 195, FH I 55, FP 214, HON 170.

Comment   One of the things we learn about life, as time passes, is that 'truth will out'. Truth seems to march on and manage to survive even when covered by lies.

Reading   What kind of liar are you?
People lie because they don't remember clearly what they saw.
People lie because they can't help making a story better than it was the way it happened.

People tell 'white lies' so as to be decent to others.
People lie in a pinch, hating to do it, but lying on
because it might be worse.
And people lie just to be liars for a crooked personal
gain.
What sort of liar are you?
Which of these liars are you?

Carl Sandburg

Comment	It is an insult to call someone a liar, but as the reading points out, most of us are guilty of telling untruths – for one reason or another – from time to time. But we should try always to be truthful; on truth trust is built.
Scripture readings	A 'Sanctify them in the truth; thy word is truth.' B 'When the spirit of truth comes, he will guide you into the truth.' C 'For this I was born and for this I have come into the world, to bear witness to the truth.' D 'Everyone who is of the truth hears my voice.' E 'You will know the truth, and the truth will make you free.'
Prayer	O God you can see my inmost thoughts and know me better than I know myself. You understand the impulses I feel, the ambitions I have, the silent loneliness I experience. Forgive me my sins against truth – the untruth within me, the half-truths, the evasions, the exaggerations, the trying silences that deceive, the masks I wear before the world. Help me to see myself as I really am, fill me with the courage I shall need if I am to seek the truth and live in truth.
Hymn	'Let all that is within me', CH 167, FH I 15, FP 159, HON 148, SLW 20.

ALTERNATIVES

Hymns	'Love is his word', CH 185, FH I 66, FP 107, HON 166, PL 75. 'Make me a channel', CH 189, FH I 35, FP 108, HON 167, SLW 97. 'He who would valiant be', CH 119, HON 105, PL 285.
Prayers	See assembly 3 or 52.

5   Personal Responsibility

Hymn	'Give me joy in my heart', CH 84, FH I 78, FP 105, HON 78, NL 63, NO 70, SLW 4.
Reading	The story is told of a king who placed a heavy stone in the road and then hid and watched to see who would remove it. Men of various classes came and worked their way round it, some loudly blaming the king for not keeping the highways clear, but all dodging the duty of getting it out of the way. At last a poor peasant on his way to town with his burden of vegetables for sale came, and, contemplating the stone, laid down his load, and rolled the stone into the gutter. Then, turning round, he spied a purse that had lain right under the stone. He opened it and found it full of gold pieces with a note from the king saying it was for the one who should remove the stone.
Comment	The poor peasant was rewarded because he took responsibility for what was wrong. If a chair falls over in class, do you pick it up, or walk round it? If an accident occurs or you do wrong, do you own up or say 'It's not my fault'?
Scripture reading	Matthew 25:14–30 or *New World*, p.84.
Comment	Reward was given according to the responsibility that each accepted.
Prayer	Give me, O Lord, a sense of responsibility. Give me a sense of responsibility to myself, so that I may not waste the gifts which you have given to me; a sense of responsibility to my parents, so that I may repay them for all the love and care they have given to me; a sense of responsibility to my school, so that all the patient teaching I have received may not be wasted;

a sense of responsibility to my friends,
so that I may not fail their trust in me.
Give me, O Lord, a sense of responsibility that I may
grow to real maturity; this I ask through Christ your
Son. Amen.

Hymn   'Walk with me, oh my Lord', CH 340, FH II 2, FP 191,
HON 292.

ALTERNATIVES

Hymns   'We are one in the Spirit', CH 342, FH I 46, HON 294, PL
296.
'Lord of all hopefulness', CH 181, HON 162, NL 54, NO
39, PL 288, SLW 44.

Prayers   See assembly 38 or 15.

6   Respect for Self

Hymn   'It's me, it's me, O Lord', CH 144, FH I 21, FP 113, HON
127.

Reading 1   I understand more and more how true Daddy's words
were when he said, 'All children must look after their
own upbringing'. Parents can only give good advice or
put them on the right paths, but the final forming of a
person's character lies in his own hands.

Diary of Anne Frank

Comment   How are you looking after yourself? Anne Frank says,
'the final forming of a person's character lies in his own
hands'. Today that forming will continue. What sort of
a person are you forming yourself into? Are you, for
example, always complaining, or are you grateful for
what you have?

Reading 2   Today upon a bus, I saw a lovely girl
with golden hair;
I envied her – she seemed so gay – and
wished I were as fair.

When suddenly she rose to leave, I saw
  her hobble down the aisle;
She had one foot and wore a crutch, but
  as she passed, a smile.
Oh, God, forgive me when I whine;
I have two feet – the world is mine!

And then I stopped to buy some sweets.
  The lad who sold them had
Such charm, I talked with him – he said
  to me:
'It's nice to talk with folks like you.
You see', he said, 'I'm blind.'
Oh, God, forgive me when I whine;
I have two eyes – the world is mine!

Then, walking down the street, I saw a
  child with eyes of blue.
He stood and watched the others play;
It seemed he knew not what to do.
I stopped for a moment, then I said:
'Why don't you join the others, dear?'
He looked ahead without a word, and then
I knew he could not hear.
Oh, God, forgive me when I whine;
I have two ears – the world is mine.

With feet to take me where I'd go,
With eyes to see the sunset's glow,
With ears to hear what I would know,
Oh, God, forgive me when I whine;
I'm blessed, indeed! The world is mine.

Anon.

Prayer

Give me a good digestion, Lord,
  And also something to digest;
Give me a healthy body, Lord,
  With sense to keep it at its best.

Give me a healthy mind, good Lord,
  To keep the good and pure in sight,
Which seeing sin is not appalled
  But finds a way to set it right.

Give me a mind that is not bored,
That does not whimper, whine or sigh;
Don't let me worry overmuch
About the fussy thing called I.

Give me a sense of humour, Lord,
Give me the grace to see a joke,
To get some happiness from life
And pass it on to other folk.

'Thank you', CH 298, FH I 95, HON 257, PL 275.

VES

'Sing my soul', CH 278, FH I 62, FP 31.
'Oh the love of my Lord', CH 231, FH I 79, FP 81, HON 195.
'May the long-time sun', FH IV 24.

See assembly 13 or 38.

Respect for Others

Hymn 'Love is his word', CH 185, FH I 66, FP 107, HON 166, PL 75.

Reading Yes, the first woman I saw I myself picked up from the street. She had been half eaten by the rats and ants. I took her to the hospital but they could not do anything for her. They only took her in because I refused to move until they accepted her. From there I went to the municipality and I asked them to give me a place where I could bring these people because on the same day I had found other people dying in the streets. The health officer of the municipality took me to the temple, the Kali Temple, and showed me the dormashalah where the people used to rest after they had done their worship of Kali goddess. It was an empty building; he asked me if I would accept it. I was very happy to have that place for many reasons, but especially knowing that it was a centre of worship and devotion of the Hindus. Within 24 hours we had our patients there and we started the work of the home for the sick and dying who are destitutes. Since then we have picked up over 23,000 people from the streets of Calcutta of which about 50 per cent have died.

Mother Teresa

Comment   Many wonderful people over the centuries have put Jesus's words into practice. Mother Teresa is one of those who has done much for others.

Scripture   John 13:33–35 or *New World*, p.397.
reading

Prayer   Litany of Caring

READER   Break down, O Lord, the wall of selfishness that cuts us off from the needs of other people. We could help them if we cared:

ALL   Teach us, O God, to care.

READER   The unpopular pupils whom we do not want to know, because we are afraid of becoming unpopular ourselves. We could help them if we cared:

ALL   Teach us, O God, to care.

READER   The dull, boring people, who are not actively disliked but simply ignored, and therefore lonely. We could help them if we cared:

ALL   Teach us, O God, to care.

READER   All those who serve us each day and whom we don't bother to treat with much courtesy, but who may be hurt by our off-handedness. We could help them if we cared:

ALL   Teach us, O God, to care.

READER   The old people who long for somebody young to talk to, but whom we prefer not to bother about because we find them tedious. We could help them if we cared:

ALL   Teach us, O God, to care.

READER   All these and many others, we have the power and opportunity to help, Lord. Your son would have used

our opportunities: teach us to use them willingly in his
name. Amen.

Hymn   'Love is something if you give it away', NL 134, NO 14.

ALTERNATIVES

Hymns   'Love is patient', FH IV 97.
'When I needed a neighbour', CH 353, FH I 41, NL 123,
NO 13, PL 298.

Prayers   Make us ever eager, Lord, to share the good things that
we have. Grant us such a measure of thy Spirit that we
may find more joy in giving than in getting. Make us
ready to give cheerfully without grudging, secretly
without praise, and in sincerity without looking for
gratitude, for Jesus Christ's sake.

John Hunter

See also assembly 16 or 14.

8   Judging Others

Hymn   'All people that on earth do dwell', AM 166, CH 10, HON
14, NL 44, PL 11.

Comment   We sang, 'All people that on earth do dwell', which of
course includes those we don't get on with, those we
look down on and make judgements about, because of
their colour, age, or beliefs.

Reading 1   The six-man crew were all regulars. Friends of many
trips. The Corporation cart made its way along the
street. Past the morning newspaper offices. Every few
feet picking up the waste of an affluent society. The
driver pulled away from the kerb and looked in his
mirror as he passed a badly parked van. Then back
along the kerb again. The driver raised the back of his
truck to bring the rubbish forward, and the children
loved it.

    The time in that narrow Belfast street was three

minutes to twelve on Monday 20 March 1972. From somewhere in a badly parked van behind the dust-cart a tiny spark jumped. A spark so small that the naked eye couldn't have seen it. And in less time than it takes to tell, the parked van exploded.

Flames leapt from her metal bodywork, flames of red, yellow, and lilac wrapped in deep grey smoke. From the Belfast Corporation dust-cart the bodies flew. People screamed. Pieces of human flesh littered the street. Some lay for ever still while others incredibly picked themselves up and staggered shocked away.

Six people died in that instant of time in Donegal Street, Belfast, on Monday 20 March 1972 at 11.57 am. Protestant and Roman Catholic, they died together as they have so often since in other outrages. Old and young; they all died together.

Robin Williamson

Comment   'All died together'. Catholics and Protestants; young and old. As Jimmy Savile says in his book *God'll Fix It* this judging of other people is 'an abuse of the mind' and there is another way to go about it.

Reading 2   On one occasion, in Stoke Mandeville Hospital, we had three people from Northern Ireland. They were in different wards. In one ward was a soldier who had been caught in gunfire and the bullet had chipped the top of his spine and rendered him paraplegic. In another ward we had a girl of 13 – a very pretty girl – who just happened to be standing on a street corner. She took a bullet through the throat and that rendered her paraplegic. In yet another ward, we had one of the militant bodies. He was actually doing the firing at the time. He was in a wheelchair. If anyone wanted to look at the futility of that particular course of action, they had only to look at those three people. Three lives were completely ruined. After a while, when they all started to recover, they all trundled their wheelchairs down to the hospital canteen. The four of us used to talk, and we had a lot to talk about. I wish you could have seen the four of us talking together. And three of them were all suffering from the same thing. Yet, would you believe it, they were the best of friends. So I was right in the first place. There is another way of doing things.

What had happened in their situation was a mental abuse and that put these people into wheelchairs. They have learned to live with their afflictions.

Jimmy Savile

Prayer   Almighty God, help us not to abuse our minds; help us not to judge others by appearances. Help us, Lord, to understand that no matter what colour we are or what age or what we believe, we are all equally your sons and daughters. May we never intentionally give hurt or offence to anyone and help us to realise that if we are all your sons and daughters that makes us brothers and sisters in your family. We ask for your help through Christ our Lord. Amen.

Hymn   'Love is his word', CH 185, FH I 66, FP 107, HON 166, PL 75.

ALTERNATIVES

Hymns   'Whatsoever you do', CH 352, FH I 71, FP 180, HON 298.
'When I needed a neighbour', CH 353, FH I 41, NL 123, NO 13, PL 298.
'Make me a channel', CH 189, FH I 35, FP 108, HON 167, SLW 97.

Prayers   See assembly 3 or 16.

9   Personal Integrity

Hymn   'Breathe on me, Breath of God', AM 236, CH 37, HON 34, NL 86, PL 6.

Comment   It is important that we grow up to be people of integrity. But what is 'integrity'? It is being true to yourself. Having high ideals and trying to live up to them. St Paul helps us to understand what it is.

Scripture reading   2 Corinthians 6:6–8 or *New World*, p.229.

Comment	A person who is trying to live sincerely understands that God knows and sees all that he or she does.
Scripture reading	Psalm 139:1–6 or, preferably, *Winding Quest*, p.402.
Prayer	O Lord and Master, you know us better than we know ourselves. Like an X-ray, your Holy Spirit can see through us and search out our weaknesses and our fears. Pour your love into our hearts that we may become the sort of people you want us to be. Amen.
Hymn	'Amazing Grace', CH 19, FH I 36, FP 73, HON 20, SLW 5.

ALTERNATIVES

Hymn	'Happy the man', CH 111, FH I 53, FP 86, HON 99.

Prayers	Through every minute of this day,
	  Be with me, Lord!
	Through every day of all this week,
	  Be with me, Lord!
	Through every week of all this year,
	  Be with me, Lord!
	Through all the years of all this life,
	  Be with me, Lord!
	So shall the days and weeks and years,
	Be threaded on a golden cord,
	And all draw on with sweet accord
	Unto thy fulness, Lord
	That so, when time is past,
	By grace, I may at last
	  Be with thee, Lord.

John Oxenham

See also assembly 4.

10   Respect for Property

Hymn	'Morning has broken', CH 196, FH I 73, FP 196, HON 171, NL 79, SLW 9.

Comment   God has given us a beautiful world to live in, but it is often cluttered up and spoilt by man. Listen now to a reading about an animal who made a mess!

Reading 1   A great writer, called Sir Osbert Sitwell, tells the story of a man who once captured a very attractive little beaver. He decided to keep it as a pet and take it to his country home. To get there he had to pass through New York and decided to spend the night there at his flat. His wife received the unexpected visitor kindly and it was decided that the best place for the animal to spend the night was in the drawing room. They placed a wooden box lined with straw in the room so that the beaver could curl up in it. They then locked the door. When they entered the room next morning they found nothing there except the beaver and a dam! The animal had got out of its box and accidentally knocked over a small table on which was a vase of flowers. The spilt water on the floor had brought all the beaver's dam-building instincts into play. It had carefully sawn up the valuable chairs and tables and with the aid of cushions and books had made a wonderful dam.

Maurice Nassan

Comment   The beaver was only acting according to his nature; it was a natural instinct that led him to destroy the furniture. We are not mere animals with an instinct to destroy. Some boys and girls act as though we are – defacing walls and desks, damaging others' clothes, dropping litter. It is a war against the beauty of God's creation, a disrespect of our surroundings. What we do to other people's property should tell us a great deal about ourselves. We are shaping ourselves in the wrong way – we are damaging ourselves as we damage things.

Reading 2   Life is like a jem* in a crown
Something more precious than the things around.
Something to care for, preserve
And keep safe.

Like a diamond is cut, so is life.
We cut our lives
But some of us cut it wrongly

So it breaks in pieces
And is scattered around
And is useless,
A precious thing gone to waste.

J. Beckett

*The spelling of the original is retained.

Prayer   Lord God, help me to respect myself. I have only one life which I can only live once. Life is precious. I am precious in your sight. Help me to remember that each person is unique and special. Help me too to respect your creation and the things of nature. Help me to respect other people's property, for you have told us that whatever we do to other people we do to you.

Hymn   'Whatsoever you do', CH 352, FH I 71, FP 180, HON 298.

ALTERNATIVES

Hymns   'All the nations', CH 12, FH I 81, FP 62, HON 17.
'All things bright and beautiful', AM 442, CH 13, HON 18.

Prayers   See assembly 51 or 38 (alternative prayer).

11   Incarnation

Hymn   'Where would we be without Christ', CH 359, FH I 74, FP 192.

Reading 1   A man who fell 170 ft down an abandoned tin mine in Cornwall survived for five days, drinking rainwater which collected at the bottom of the shaft.

He was rescued late last night and walked away into the night cheerful and apparently unscathed.

Firemen, police and coastguards who took part in the rescue were surprised that 50-year-old John Elmes, a Londoner without a settled home, was found. The shaft is at Kenidjack, an area near St Just, close to Land's End, which is honeycombed with disused mines. It is shunned by local people.

Yesterday three boys collecting firewood for a camp fire threw a stone down the shaft and heard Mr Elmes calling.

He was brought to the surface strapped to a fireman who had been lowered down the mine.

He believes that the shaft was on a slight slope and that he bounced from side to side as he tumbled to the bottom.

Anon.

Comment

Five days in darkness . . . in fear of your life! Mankind was cut off from God, rather like that, before Jesus came as the Light of the World.

Reading 2

'The Light of the World' is the title of a famous picture by Holman Hunt painted in 1854. It portrays Christ, thorn-crowned, and carrying a lantern, knocking at a closed door. When the artist showed the completed picture to some friends, one pointed out what seemed to be an omission. 'You have put no handle on the door', he said to Holman Hunt. The artist replied, 'We must open to the Light – the handle is on the inside'.

Anon.

Prayer

Lord God, our need of you is greater than we know or express; do not wait, do not delay, but come quickly to our aid.

As you come to us, Lord, bring us forgiveness; we are ungrateful to those who love us; we are indifferent to the needs of others; where we see injustice we do not protest; help us to love others with the love you have shown us.

Bring us peace that we may meet difficulties and disappointments with calm and courage.

Bring us joy, because God has become man so that all men may be again free of darkness, free of fear, as members of the family of God. Amen.

Hymn

'The Virgin Mary had a baby boy', CH 321, FH I 88, FP 147, HON 275, PL 156.

ALTERNATIVES

Hymns
'Lord Jesus Christ', CH 179, FH I 100, FP 181, HON 159.
'Every star shall sing a carol', NL 8, NO 5, PL 154.
'Colours of day', CH 45, FH II 1, FP 9, HON 42.

Prayers
See assembly 16, 15 or 35.

12   The Gift of Love

Hymn
'We three Kings of Orient are', CH 349, HON 297.

Comment
'Bearing gifts' the Wise Men, or Magi, came to the stable where Jesus was born.

Scripture reading
Matthew 2:1–12.

Reading
Didst Thou, Lord Jesus, play with toys
Like other little girls and boys;
A lamb Thy mother made with care
From bits of wool she had to spare?
And didst Thou gurgle with delight
And have it in Thy cot at night?

Did Joseph, of a winter's night,
Sit whittling by the fire's light,
The day's work done, all else was dark,
And make for Thee a Noah's ark,
A sturdy ship of wood and glue,
And wooden creatures, two by two?

The Magi, seeking Thee from far,
Who found Thee by the wandering star,
Brought gifts, such costly gifts they were,
Of gold and frankincense and myrrh;
Then Thou didst bless their will to please,
But couldst not play with gifts like these.

What, then O Jesus, should I bring
In homage to my infant King?
The poorest present, so I'm told

If given from the heart, is gold
And fragrant as the frankincense
When love is not the least expense.

Then token be the gift I bear
Of lasting loving like the myrrh.

Killian Twell, OFM

Prayer

Eternal God, we thank you for showing yourself to us in Jesus Christ; help us now to prepare to celebrate his birth with joy.

We thank you for the birth, childhood and manhood of Jesus; may we find in each moment of his life the revelation of your love for us.

We pray that Christ may become alive in each one of us, so that through us his love may be visible to all men.

We pray at this time for the world, where love and justice struggle against war and oppression, wastefulness and extravagance.

May the love of the Lord Jesus draw us to himself;

May the power of the Lord Jesus strengthen us in his service;

May the joy of the Lord Jesus fill our hearts.

Hymn

'Give me joy in my heart', CH 84, FH I 78, FP 105, HON 78, NL 63, NO 70, SLW 4.

ALTERNATIVES

Hymns

'Come love carolling', NL 7.

'Every star shall sing a carol', NL 8, NO 5, PL 154.

Prayers

God, this is your world,
You made us,
You love us;
Teach us how to live
In the world that you have made.

Hope Freeman

See also assembly 21.

13   Dignity of the Individual

Hymn   'In the bleak mid-winter', AM 67, CH 137, HON 123.

Comment   The last verse of that carol is rather beautiful and full of
               meaning! 'What can I give him . . . yet what I can I give
               him – give my heart.' Our reading today is about a little
               boy that gave what was most dear to him.

Reading   One Christmas, Santa Claus brought me a toy engine. I
               took it with me to the convent, and played with it while
               mother and the nuns discussed old times. But it was a
               young nun who brought us in to see the crib. When I
               saw the Holy Child in the manger I was distressed
               because little as I had, he had nothing at all. For me it
               was fresh proof of the incompetence of Santa Claus. I
               asked the young nun politely if the Holy Child didn't
               like toys, and she replied composedly enough: 'Oh he
               does, but his mother is too poor to afford them'. That
               settled it. My mother was poor too, but at Christmas
               she at least managed to buy me something even if it was
               only a box of crayons. I distinctly remember getting
               into the crib and putting the engine between his out-
               stretched arms. I probably showed him how to wind it
               as well, because a small baby like that would not be
               clever enough to know. I remember too the tearful
               feeling of reckless generosity with which I left him
               there in the nightly darkness of the chapel, clutching
               my toy engine to his chest.

                                                        Frank O'Connor

Comment   Our dignity as persons rests more on what we are than
               on what we have.

Prayer   I asked God for strength that I might achieve;
               I was made weak that I might learn humbly to obey.

               I asked for help that I might do greater things;
               I was given infirmity that I might do better things.

               I asked for riches that I might be happy;
               I was given poverty that I might be wise.

I asked for all things that I might enjoy life;
I was given life that I might enjoy all things.

I was given nothing that I asked for;
But everything that I had hoped for.

Despite myself, my prayers were answered;
I am among all men most richly blessed.

Anon.

Hymn   'Come, come, come to the manger', CH 48, HON 45.

ALTERNATIVES

Hymns   'See amid the winter's snow', HON 236, PL 144.
'Sing high with the holly', NL 18.
'No use knocking on the window', NL 19.

Prayers   See assembly 15 or 14.

14   Christ's Sacrifice

Hymn   'Lord of the dance' (first three verses), CH 131, FH I 68, NL 28, NO 54, PL 92.

Reading   During a cruel and bloody war, a commander took an oath in the presence of his troops that he would slaughter the entire population of a certain town, and in due course the bloodhounds of war were let loose on the defenceless people.

Now it so happened that a fugitive, seeking for a shelter, saw a sight which was indirectly the means of saving both his own life and the lives of others. He spied a number of soldiers as they broke into a house, the inmates of which they put to the sword. On leaving it, they fastened up the place again, and one of them, dipping a cloth in a pool of blood, splashed it on the door, as a token to any who might follow of what had taken place inside.

Quick as his feet could carry him, the poor fugitive sped away to a large house in the centre of the town where a number of his friends were concealed, and breathlessly told them what he had seen. At once it flashed upon them how to act. A goat was in the yard. It was immediately killed, and its blood splashed on the door. Scarcely could they close the door again when a band of soldiers rushed into the street and began to slay right and left. But when they came to the blood-marked door they made no attempt to enter.

The sword – so they thought – had already entered and performed its work in that house. Thus, while the many around were put to death, all inside the blood-sprinkled door were saved.

                                                                Anon.

Comment   The blood sprinkled on the door saved the people hiding in the house. Just as the angel of death passed over the houses where the Hebrews had marked their door posts with blood.

Scripture   Exodus 12:21–27 or *Winding Quest*, p.103.
reading

Comment   It was the very night when Jesus and his friends were celebrating the Passover – the anniversary of the night when Moses and the Hebrews had escaped slavery in Egypt – that Jesus went out to his death. The shedding of his blood saved us from death.

Hymn   Last two verses of 'Lord of the dance'.

Prayer   Thanks be to thee, our Lord Jesus Christ, for all the benefits which thou hast given us; for all the pains and insults which thou hast borne for us.

O most merciful redeemer, friend and brother, may we know thee more clearly, love thee more dearly and follow thee more nearly, now and ever.

                                              St Richard of Chichester

ALTERNATIVES

Hymns   'It was on a Friday morning', NL 34.
                'Where would we be without Christ', CH 359, FH I 74, FP 192.

'Were you there', CH 347, FH I 99, FP 40, HON 296, PL 190.

Prayers   See assembly 16 or 1 (alternative prayer).

15   Risen Lord

Hymn   'Morning has broken', CH 196, FH I 73, FP 196, HON 171, NL 79, SLW 9.

Comment   If you wake in the middle of the night, you know that no matter how dark it is, how still all around seems, how dead all living things appear – the morning will come and light will overcome darkness.

Reading
At three o'clock in the morning if you
    open your window and listen
You will hear the feet of the wind that
    is going to call the sun,
And the trees in the darkness rustle,
And the trees in the moonlight glisten,
And though it is deep dark night, you
    know that the night is done.

                                        Anon.

Scripture reading   John 20:1–18 or *New World*, p.407.

Comment   Christ said 'I am the Light of the World' and his rising from the dead is a victory for light over darkness, goodness over evil, life over death.

Prayer
O thou who art the light of the minds that know thee;
    the life of the souls that love thee;
    and the strength of the wills that serve thee;
Help us to know thee that we may truly love thee;
    so to love thee that we may fully serve thee;
    whom to serve is perfect freedom;
    through Jesus Christ our Lord.

                            Gelasian Sacramentary

Hymn   'Now the green blade riseth', CH 53, FH II 14, HON 181,
                NL 36, PL 201.

ALTERNATIVES

Hymns   'Bring all you dear-bought nations', CH 38, HON 35.
                'Lord of the dance', CH 131, FH I 68, NL 28, NO 54,
                PL 92.
                'Christ the Lord is risen', AM 131, CH 44, HON 41, PL
                192.

Prayer   See assembly 43.

16   Living Lord

Hymn   'Let all that is within me', CH 167, FH I 15, FP 159, HON
                148, SLW 20.

Reading   Elizabeth Pilenko was a well-educated Russian,
                brought up in a rich family owning land in the south of
                Russia. During the Revolution she supported those
                who were trying to obtain justice for the peasants. A
                few years later she settled in Paris and there became a
                Christian. She founded a convent and, as Mother
                Maria, she spent herself in caring for the Russian
                refugees who fled to France to escape the violence of
                the revolutionaries.

    In 1940 France became an occupied country. Mother
                Maria opened the doors of her convent as a haven for
                Jews persecuted by the German army of occupation.
                She knew the risks she was running. After a month of
                helping hundreds of Jews to escape to safety, the Ges-
                tapo arrived at the convent. Mother Maria was arrested
                and sent to the concentration camp at Ravensbruck.

    Here she continued to give herself unceasingly for
                the suffering prisoners. Even the guards acknowledged
                her goodness, calling her 'that wonderful Russian nun'.
                After she had spent two and a half years in the camp a
                new block of buildings went up. The prisoners were
                told that they were hot baths. In fact, they were gas
                chambers where mass execution of prisoners would
                take place.

One day a few dozen women prisoners were lined up by the guards outside the new buildings. One of the girls in the line became hysterical. Mother Maria was not one of those chosen to enter the buildings. She came up to the girl and said, 'Don't be frightened. Look, I shall take your turn.' In line with the rest, she passed through the door. It was Good Friday, 1945.

Frances Stantan

Comment   It is hardly likely that we will ever have the opportunity to give our lives for another person, but we do have the daily opportunity of living for others – helping others.

Prayer   Christ has
no body on earth but yours;
no hands but yours
no feet but yours.
Yours are the eyes
through which is to look out
Christ's compassion to the world.
Yours are the feet
with which he is to go about
doing good.
Yours are the hands
with which he is to bless men now.

Hymn   'Whatsoever you do', CH 352, FH I 71, FP 180, HON 298.

ALTERNATIVES

Hymns   'All glory, praise and honour', AM 98, CH 8, HON 10, PL 184.
'At the name of Jesus', AM 225, CH 28, FH II 81, HON 27, NL 136, SLW 45.

Prayers   See assembly 35 or 19.

17   Pentecost – Fire of the Spirit

Comment   'Fire.' If someone rushed in here now calling, 'fire, fire', we would put our fire drill into operation. If we

didn't lives might be at risk. Listen now to the words of
a ballad by Fred Dallas about a terrible fire that raged
for four days in 1958 in Smithfield Market, London.

Reading

On the coldest day in all the year,
   it was a Thursday morning,
and the hottest place in London
   was the Smithfield Market burning.
It burned four days without a pause,
   it melted all the snow;
and two brave men were choked to death,
   trapped in the smoke below.
They died there down below.

It was down there underneath the ground
   the fire it started burning,
it raged along each storage hall
   and round each passage turning.
The melted fat flared in the fire
   and filled the air with smoke.
The firemen they wore gas masks
   for fear that they would choke,
down in the terrible smoke.

Ten minutes was the longest time
   that they could stay down there,
for the heat and the fumes and the burning fat
   was more than they could bear;
but two men lost their way below
   and lay down there to die.
The searchers found them, but too late
   to lead them to the sky.
They laid them 'neath the sky.

Another day had passed
   when an explosion rocked the town.
The fire broke out into the air
   and Smithfield towers came down.
One hundred feet into the air
   and burning flames leapt high.
From Clerkenwell to London Bridge
   we saw them in the sky.
They lit up all the sky.

From every London fire brigade,
  they came to fight the flames.
A thousand firemen heroes
  and we don't know all their names;
but two men died and two wives cried,
  and three young children too.
Remember them and all the men
  who fight the fires for you,
who die in the fires for you.

Fred Dallas

Comment

Fire does not, of course, just kill and destroy. It can give light and comfort; it can warm, protect, and cleanse. It is not surprising that the Holy Spirit used fire as a symbol of its presence.

Scripture readings

A There God appeared to Moses in the shape of a flame of fire, coming from the middle of a bush.

Exodus 3:2

B Moses led the people of the camp to meet God; and they stood at the bottom of the mountain. The mountain of Sinai was entirely wrapped in smoke, because God had descended on it in the form of fire.

Exodus 19:18

C When Pentecost day came round, they had all met in one room, when suddenly they heard what sounded like a powerful wind from heaven, the noise of which filled the entire house in which they were sitting, and something appeared to them that seemed like tongues of fire, these separated and came to rest on the head of each of them.

Acts 2:3

Prayer

O God our Father, we thank you for fire. It warms us, comforts us and can provide light for us. May the fire of your Holy Spirit warm our hearts, comfort us when we are lonely and worried and light up our minds and hearts. Amen.

Hymn

'Colours of day', CH 45, FH II 1, FP 9, HON 42.

ALTERNATIVES

Hymns	'Holy spirit of fire', CH 125, FH II 7, FP 90.
	'Holy Spirit, Lord of light', CH 124, HON 109, PL 216.
Prayer	See assembly 15.

18   Pentecost – The Symbol of Wind

Hymn	'Come Holy Ghost', CH 50, HON 48, PL 8 (first four verses).
Reading	Rumbling in the chimneys,
	Rattling at the doors,
	Round the roofs and round the roads
	The rude wind roars;
	Raging through the darkness,
	Raving through the trees,
	Racing off again across
	The great grey seas.

Rodney Bennett

Comment	On a stormy night the wind can fill us with fear. Sometimes we read or hear about hurricanes that tear up houses and toss cars and people about. God has in the past used the symbol of wind for the power of his presence.
Scripture readings	A Exodus 14:19–22 or *Winding Quest*, p.106.
	B 1 Kings 19:9–24 or *Winding Quest*, p.228.
Comment	When God's Spirit came upon the first followers of Jesus at Pentecost time, his approach was announced by the blowing of a strong wind.
Scripture reading	C Acts 2:1–4 or *New World*, p.163.
Prayer	May the strength of God pilot us.
	May the power of God preserve us.
	May the wisdom of God instruct us.
	May the hand of God protect us.

May the way of God direct us.
May the shield of God defend us,
May the host of God guard us against the snares of
    evil and the temptations of the world.

St Patrick's Breastplate

Hymn   'Come Holy Ghost', CH 50, HON 48, PL 8 (last three
verses).

ALTERNATIVES

Readings   See assembly 20.

Hymns   'Holy Spirit, Lord of Light', CH 124, HON 109, PL 216.
'Where does the wind come from?', CH 357, FH II 89.
'God's Spirit is in my heart', CH 99, FH I 57, FP 35, HON
89, NL 116, SLW 93.

Prayers   See assembly 15 or 25.

19   Pentecost – Breath of God

Hymn   'Breathe on me, breath of God', AM 236, CH 37, HON
34, NL 86, PL 6.

Comment   The greatest thing that God ever did – and carries on
doing – was to make the Universe – all stars and
planets, seas and oceans, plants and animals. Finally he
made something in his own image – man.

Reading   God created the world and set man in it and he loved
him.
Up from the bed of the river
God scooped the clay,
and by the bank of the river
he kneeled him down.
And there the great God almighty,
who lit the sun and fixed it in the sky,
who flung the stars to the most far corner of night,
who rounded the earth in the middle of his hand,
this great God,

like a mother bending over her baby,
kneeled down in the dust,
toiling over a lump of clay
till he shaped it in his own image.
There into it he blew the breath of life
and man became a living soul.

James Weldon Johnson

Comment	Listen now to two short Bible readings. The first should help you to understand the second.
Scripture readings	A Ezekiel 37:1–10. B John 20:19–23.
Comment	It was because the Apostles were lifeless – full of fear and anxiety that Jesus needed to breathe on them and fill them with his brave Spirit. After they had received the Holy Spirit the first thing they did was to go out into the streets to tell people the truth about Jesus.
Prayer	Lord, be with us this day. Within us to purify us; Above us to draw us up; Beneath us to sustain us; Before us to lead us; Behind us to restrain us; Around us to protect us.　　　　St Patrick
Hymn	'Colours of day', CH 45, FH II 1, FP 9, HON 42.

ALTERNATIVES

Hymns	'Sing my soul', CH 278, FH I 62, FP 31. 'Oh the love of my Lord', CH 231, FH I 79, FP 81, HON 195. 'Come Holy Ghost', CH 50, HON 48, PL 8.
Prayers	See assembly 15 or 13.

20　　The Holy Trinity

Hymn	'Holy, holy, holy! Lord God', AM 160, CH 123, HON 107, PL 222.

Comment Christian teaching about the Holy Trinity is one of the most important but one of the most difficult for us to grasp. Here are some words from Jimmy Savile about the Trinity.

Reading I believe that people latch on to different parts of the God family to suit themselves. After all, all Christian beliefs that are formulated in this sort of way – like the Holy Trinity – are only the ways that men and women have of describing God.

When the Fathers of the early church wanted to find some words to describe God, they came up with the Holy Trinity. It's all a bit mathematical. That sort of formula might put people off. As far as I'm concerned, the Holy Trinity means that God is in one lump! It is just God's three ways of being God. I can't say I think a lot about the Holy Trinity or about God the Holy Spirit, because my religion is very much a practical religion, although I do have a great sense of history and tradition. If you feel more at home talking about God the Holy Spirit, then use that. After all, the Holy Spirit, I think, is just another way of talking about the spirit of Jesus.

Jimmy Savile

Comment Jimmy is wrong about one thing. It does seem mathematical – but it isn't nor is there any likelihood of the number of persons changing. It's more like God's intimate family life, where total love is the bond and uniting force between the persons of the Trinity. God is one, and, he has told us, 'God is all love'. Love unites and total love unites totally.

Scripture readings A Do you not believe that I am in the Father and the Father is in me?

John 14:10

B If anyone loves me he will keep my word, and my Father will love him, and we shall come to him and make our home with him.

John 14:23

C Anyone who fails to love can never have known God, because God is love.

1 John 4:8

D   No one has ever seen God; but as long as we love one another God will live in us and his love will be complete in us. We can know that we are living in him and he is living in us because he lets us share his Spirit.

1 John 4:12–13

Prayer   All our prayers, Almighty Father, are offered to you through your Son Jesus Christ. Fill us with your Holy Spirit, so that with a deeper love and trust in you we may build up our Christian life with more frequent prayer. This we ask, in the Holy Spirit and through Jesus, your Son. Amen.

Hymn   'Love is his word', CH 185, FH I 66, FP 107, HON 166, PL 75.

ALTERNATIVES

Hymns   'Sing my soul', CH 278, FH I 62, FP 31.
'Oh the love of my Lord', CH 231, FH I 79, FP 81, HON 195.
'Firmly I believe', AM 186, CH 75, HON 70, PL 219.

Prayers   I bind unto myself today
The Power of God to hold and lead,
His eye to watch, his might to stay,
His ear to harken to my need;
The wisdom of my God to teach,
His hand to guide, his shield to ward;
The word of God to give me speech,
His heavenly host to be my guard.

St Patrick

See also assembly 25.

21   Vocation

Hymn   'Follow me', HON 71.

Scripture reading   1 Samuel 3:3–11.

Comment	Christ called men and women to follow him in the New Testament. Some answered – some didn't.
Scripture readings	A Matthew 9:9. B Matthew 4:18–19. C Matthew 19:16–22.
Comment	The Apostles left their jobs and followed Jesus. The rich young man was called too, but there was an obstacle in the way to his joining Christ. Jesus calls us – what do we put in the way of following him more faithfully?
Prayer	Dear Lord Jesus, teach us to be generous, to serve you as you deserve, to give and not to count the cost, to fight and not to heed the wounds, to toil and not to seek for rest, to labour and ask for no reward save that of knowing that we do your will. Amen.

St Ignatius Loyola

Hymn	'Amazing Grace', CH 19, FH I 36, FP 73, HON 20, SLW 5.

ALTERNATIVES

Hymns	'Let all that is within me', CH 167, FH I 15, FP 159, HON 148, SLW 20. 'Where would we be without Christ', CH 359, FH I 74, FP 192. 'Who would true valour see', AM 293, NL 112, NO 61.
Prayers	O Lord Jesus Christ, who art the way, the truth and the life, we pray thee suffer us not to stray from thee, who art the way, nor to distrust thee, who art the truth, nor to rest on any other than thee, who art the life. Teach us what to believe, what to do and wherein to take our rest.

Erasmus

See also assembly 43.

22   Baptism

Hymn	'One more step', NO 35.
Reading 1	St Louis of France used to sign his documents not 'Louis IX, King' but 'Louis of Poissy'. Someone asked him why, and he answered: 'Poissy is the place where I was baptised. I think more of the place where I was baptised than of Rheims Cathedral where I was crowned. It is a greater thing to be a child of God than to be the ruler of a Kingdom: this last I shall lose at death, but the other will be my passport to an everlasting glory.'

Anon.

Comment	King Louis knew where he was baptised; do you know where and when you became a child of God? Do you realise the importance of that day?
Reading 2	When the Roman youth reached manhood, he put on the *toga virilis*, the robe of manhood. The day was one of special ceremonial, a great day for him.
	When the Hindu youths of certain castes reach manhood, they put on the Yagnopavitam or sacred cord. The day is one of special ceremonial, a great day for the youth who is invested with the sacred cord.
	So the believer at his baptism acknowledges that he has 'put on Christ' – a new robe of righteousness to display to the world, a new cord of holiness that links him with the holiness of his God, a 'Holy Father'.

Anon.

Prayer	Almighty Father, at my baptism I became a child of God – your child. You adopted me into your family, the family of God. Help me to understand the importance of that wonderful event; help me to live up to the dignity expected of a child of God; help me to avoid anything that might bring disgrace to the name 'Christian'. Please give me this help through Christ your Son. Amen.
Hymn	'The Lord's my shepherd', CH 312, HON 267, NL 92, PL 115, SLW 102.

ALTERNATIVES

Hymns   'Firmly I believe', AM 186, CH 75, HON 70, PL 219.
'Immortal, invisible', AM 372, CH 134, HON 121, NL 77.
'Love is his word', CH 185, FH I 66, FP 107, HON 166, PL 75.

Prayers   See assembly 25 or 21 (alternative prayer).

23   The Eucharist

Hymn   'Love is his word', CH 185, FH I 66, FP 107, HON 166, PL 75.

Comment   In the name of love people will dare anything, willingly placing their lives at risk.

Reading   Stories continue to come out of China, from time to time, of the heroic efforts of the few remaining bishops and priests to keep the faith alive and nourish the underground Church. One such story tells of a priest who lives and works as a coolie. By means of pre-arranged sign language he gets messages around of where he is to be found – usually in the corner of a local market ostensibly selling soap. Customers who, like the early Christians, give a secret sign, are given a piece of soap, between the wrappings of which is hidden a small wafer of consecrated bread. The Chinese Christian takes his purchase home and usually after a short family service receives Communion.

Anon.

Comment   Why, throughout the centuries, have men and women risked imprisonment, torture and death to receive such a small thing – a consecrated piece of bread.

Scripture reading   1 Corinthians 11:23–25.

Comment   To do what Christ did, to share what he shared, at his last meal with his friends, is for Christians an expression of their love for their saviour.

Prayer   Almighty Father, love is expressed in giving and your Son shows you perfect love by giving himself to you, in perfect obedience. Out of love he offers himself to us too in Holy Communion. May we take every opportunity of accepting the gift he offers us and may we grow in your love to become more and more like Jesus Christ your Son, this we ask through him. Amen.

Hymn   'Take our bread we ask you', CH 297, FH I 90, FP 186, HON 256.

ALTERNATIVES

Hymns   'O Bread of Heaven', CH 213, HON 183, PL 76.
'God is love', CH 97, FP 43, HON 87, NL 132, NO 34, PL 276.

Prayers   O Lord our God, grant us grace to desire thee with our whole heart, so that desiring thee we may seek and find thee; and so finding thee, may love thee; and loving thee, may hate those sins which separate us from thee, for the sake of Jesus Christ.

St Anselm

See also assembly 14.

24   Faith

Hymn   'Do not worry', CH 63, FH I 33, FP 143, HON 61.

Reading   One of the stories told of a persecution in China in the old days is about a Chinese Christian lad named Paul Moy. He was dragged before the local mandarin, who tried to induce him to renounce the Christian faith. Other persuasions having failed, the mandarin tried bribery, and promised the boy a purse of silver.

'I thank your Excellency, but a purse of silver is not enough.'

'Very well: I will give you a purse of gold.'

'Excellency, that is still not enough.'

The magistrate had not expected such obstinate bargaining on the part of one so young and was rather annoyed.

'Well, what do you want, then?'

'Most noble Excellency, if you ask me to renounce the Faith you will have to give me enough to buy a new soul.'

He completed his glorious witness when he was beheaded a few days later.

Anon.

Comment   Such courage needs not just faith in the sense of a strong belief, but faith in the sense of tremendous trust in God's loving care of us.

Prayer   Lord, give me faith! – to live from day to day,
With tranquil heart to do my simple part,
And, with my hand in thine, just go thy way.

Lord, give me faith! – to trust, if not to know,
With quiet mind in all things thee to find,
And, child-like, go where thou wouldst have me go.

Lord give me faith! – to leave it all to thee,
The future is thy gift, I would not lift
The veil thy love has hung 'twixt it and me.

John Oxenham

Hymn   'Lord of all hopefulness', CH 181, HON 162, NL 54, NO 39, PL 288, SLW 44.

ALTERNATIVES

Hymns   'Firmly I believe and truly', AM 186, CH 75, HON 70, PL 219.
'Immortal, invisible', AM 372, CH 134, HON 121, NL 77.

Prayer   See assembly 13.

25   Mission

Hymn   'God's spirit is in my heart', CH 99, FH I 57, FP 35, HON 89, NL 116, SLW 93.

Scripture reading	Luke 4:16–22 or *New World*, p.134.
Comment	Jesus had a mission in life to accomplish; we have just heard how he first announced that mission. He called others to help him.
Scripture reading	Matthew 10:1–10 or *New World*, p.12.
Comment	The friends Jesus sent out to continue his work had to face much hardship. This, for example, is what Paul had to suffer.
Scripture reading	2 Corinthians 11:23–28 or *New World*, p.222.

Prayer

Go forth into the world in peace,
Be of good courage;
Hold fast that which is good;
Render to no man evil for evil;
Strengthen the faint-hearted;
Support the weak;
Help the afflicted;
Honour all men;
Love and serve the Lord,
Rejoicing in the power of the Holy Spirit.
And the blessing of God almighty,
The Father, the Son and the Holy Spirit
Be upon us and remain with us for ever. Amen.

From an alternative order of Confirmation in the Prayer Book as proposed in 1928.

Hymn	'Colours of day', CH 45, FH II 1, FP 9, HON 42.

ALTERNATIVES

Hymns	'Haul, haul away', CH 114, FH I 37, FP 33.
	'Forth in thy name', AM 336, CH 79, NL 109, PL 87.
Prayer	See assembly 1 (alternative prayer).

26   Trust in God

Hymn   'O Lord, my God', CH 227, FH II 27, FP 8, HON 202.

Comment   One of the mysteries of God is how he is infinite, all mighty and perfect in every way, but at the same time very close to us, wanting us to trust in him.

Reading   Bruce Larson tells a story in his book *Edge of Adventure*. It's about a letter found in a baking-powder tin wired to the handle of an old pump which offered the only hope of drinking water on a very long and seldom-used trail across the Amargosa Desert, in the USA; the letter read as follows:

'This pump is all right as of June 1932. I put the new leather sucker washer into it, and it ought to last several years. But this leather washer dries out and the pump has got to be primed. Under the white rock, I buried a bottle of water. There's enough water in it to prime the pump, but not if you drink some first. Pour in about one-quarter, and let her to wet the leather. Then pour in the rest, medium fast, and pump like crazy. You'll get water. The well has never run dry. Have faith. When you get watered up, fill the bottle and put it back like you found it for the next feller.

(signed) Desert Pete.

P.S. Don't go drinking up the water first. *Prime the pump* with it first, and you'll get all you can hold.'

Hymn   'Love is something if you give it away', NL 134, NO 14.

Comment   If we trust and leave ourselves and everything that concerns us in the hands of our loving God, that confidence will always be rewarded.

Prayer   Father, I place myself lovingly, confidently in your hands. Do with me what you will. You have made me, you know me better than I know myself – what have I to fear, if I place all my trust in you? Please hear my prayer through Christ your Son. Amen.

Hymn   'Do not worry', CH 63, FH I 33, FP 143, HON 61.

ALTERNATIVES

Hymns	'Lead us, heavenly Father, lead us', AM 311, CH 165, PL 112.
	'Lord of all hopefulness', CH 181, HON 162, NL 54, NO 39, PL 288.
Prayer	See assembly 24.

27   Conscience

Hymn	'Give joy in my heart', CH 84, FH I 78, FP 105, HON 78, NL 63, NO 70, SLW 4.
Comment	There will be joy in our hearts if we have clear consciences. There will be peace in our hearts if our consciences are at ease because we are trying to love in the right way. That means not turning our love in on ourselves but out towards others.
Reading	King Oswin was troubled to think of Bishop Aidan's long journeys on foot on the rough roads and among the stony crags of Yorkshire, and he knew that the Bishop must often find it difficult to cross the rivers, for there were few bridges. So he gave him a fine horse with royal trappings, to help him on his journeys. One day as Aidan was riding the horse over the moorlands he met a beggar who asked for alms. At once he dismounted and gave the horse to the poor man, and went on his way on foot. This was told to the king, who felt rather hurt that Aidan should have given away the horse he had particularly chosen for him as a gift. As they were going into dinner he said to him: 'Have I not many less valuable horses which might have been given to the beggar?' And Aidan, who was ever a friend of the poor, replied with his ready wit: 'What sayest thou, King? Is that son of a mare more precious in thy sight than the son of God?'
	They went into the hall, and Aidan took his place at the table, but the king, who had been out hunting, stood warming himself at the fire with his attendants.

Suddenly he ungirded his sword and threw himself at Aidan's feet, asking his forgiveness.

'I will never speak any more of this', he said, 'nor will I ever judge what, or how much, you shall give to the sons of God.'

Phyllis Garlick

Comment   Even a great king can and must respond to his conscience. We must always listen and be guided by it.

Prayer   O thou who are the light of the minds that know thee;
    the life of the souls that love thee;
    and the strength of the wills that serve thee;
Help us so to know thee that we may truly love thee;
    so to love thee that we may fully serve thee;
    whom to serve is perfect freedom;
    through Jesus Christ our Lord.

Gelasian Sacramentary

(This prayer is also used at assembly 15)

Hymn   'The King of love my shepherd is', AM 197, CH 311, HON 265, PL 114.

ALTERNATIVES

Hymns   'All you who seek a comfort sure', AM 104, CH 15, PL 176.
'Christ be beside me', CH 41, FH II 13, FP 160, HON 39.
'Where would we be', CH 359, FH I 74, FP 192.

Prayers   See assembly 57 or 23 (alternative prayer).

28   Courage

Hymn   'Lead us, heavenly Father, lead us', AM 311, CH 165, PL 112.

Reading   In one of the terrible concentration camps of the Second World War there was a Polish priest, called Father Kolbe. He had been put there because he had published comments about the Nazi regime. One of the prisoners escaped from the camp and the camp commandant, to punish the prisoners, ordered ten of them to be starved to death. Among the prisoners was a young man who had a wife and children. When the prisoners' numbers were called out, Father Kolbe stepped forward and insisted on taking the young man's place. In the death cell Father Kolbe helped the others prepare for death; he was the last to die. Because he had taken too long they injected poison into his arm. After his death, if you had gone into his cell, you would have seen a picture of Jesus on the cross scratched on the wall with his nails.

Anon.

Comment Courage like that shown in the story we have just heard is only rarely necessary, but we all quite often have to show courage in small things. Jesus showed us how to be brave.

Scripture reading John 18:1–12 or *New World*, p.400.

Prayer Lord Jesus, in the garden you were faced with the fear of suffering and death. You did what you have told us to do when faced with fear and suffering. You prayed. You were supported by your Father's love, wanting only to do what he asked of you. Your trust and confidence in God was rewarded. You rose from the dead, our Saviour and Lord. Now you support us when we are anxious and afraid. Give us courage in both the big and small things of life; help us always to seek to do your will. Amen.

Hymn 'Lord of the dance', CH 131, FH I 68, NL 28, PL 92.

ALTERNATIVES

Hymns 'Lord of all hopefulness', CH 181, HON 162, NL 54, NO 39, PL 288, SLW 44.
'Do not worry', CH 63, FH I 33, FP 143, HON 61.
'We shall overcome', CH 348, FH I 31, FP 163.

Prayers See assembly 14 or 3.

29   Confidence in God

Hymn   'Happy the man', CH 111, FH I 53, FP 86, HON 99.

Scripture reading   Mark 4:35–41 or *New World*, p.13.

Comment   This is one of the few times – except at the end of Jesus's life when they were so frightened that they ran away – when we hear that the friends of Jesus were afraid. The storm must have been tremendous for experienced fishermen to have feared for their lives.

Scripture reading   Matthew 6:23–24 or *New World*, p.97.

Prayer   Lord Jesus, I have watched the sea when I have been to the coast on holiday.
Even in summer, the waves pound the beach and hiss over the shingle
As if they were living, angry things.

I have watched the sea on the television news in winter
When great breakers have pounded the promenades
And tossed cars about as if with a giant hand.

I'm always a bit afraid of the sea, Lord,
Even in its summer moods.

Yet you could stand erect in a heaving boat
And command the tumbling waves to be still.
No wonder your disciples were amazed.
What courage you showed!

Please share that courage with me, Lord Jesus.
Great waves of temptation beat against the shores of my heart.
Help me to still their storm,
And bring me to the safe harbour of your peace.

Mary Drewery

Hymn   'Walk with me, oh my Lord', CH 340, FH II 2, FP 191, HON 292.

ALTERNATIVES

Hymns   'Do not worry', CH 63, FH I 33, FP 143, HON 61.
'Lead us, heavenly Father, lead us', AM 311, CH 165, PL 112.

Prayers   See assembly 1 (alternative prayer) or 9 (alternative prayer).

30   No Trust in Riches

Hymn   'He's got the whole world in his hand', CH 117, FH I 29, FP 58, NO 86.

Comment   Today we have two readings about people who put money first in their lives.

Reading 1   A miser in France used to keep all his gold and precious things in a cellar under the floor of his house. One day he went down through a secret trap-door at the top of the cellar to gloat over his treasure. Then the trap-door banged down so that he could not get out. No one in the house knew about the cellar and the miser could not be found. People searched all over the place without finding him. After a long time they gave up and the house was sold. The new people who bought the house wanted some new building done and the cellar was found. When it was opened the miser was found sitting at the table with all his gold glittering around him. The dead man had even eaten a candle before dying of hunger.

Maurice Nassan

Reading 2   One summer afternoon a steamer, crowded with passengers, many of them miners from California, suddenly struck a submerged wreck as it sped down the Mississippi. In a moment her deck was a wild confusion. The boats were able to take off only one-fourth of the passengers: the rest, divesting themselves of their garments, succeeded in swimming to shore. Immediately after the last had quitted the vessel, a man appeared on deck. Seizing a spar, he leapt into the river but instantly sank like a stone. When his body was recovered, it was found that, while the other passengers were escaping, he had been rifling the miners' trunks, and round his waist he had fastened bags of gold. In a quarter of an hour he had amassed more than most men do in a lifetime; but he lost himself in an instant.

Anon.

Comment   Jesus had something to say about people who put their trust in money and not in him.

Scripture readings   A   Jesus said 'How hard it is for those who have riches to enter the kingdom of God.'

Mark 10:23

B   'It is easier for a camel to pass through the eye of a needle than for a rich man to enter the kingdom of God.'

Mark 10:26

C   'Do not store up treasures for yourselves on earth, where moths and woodworms destroy them and thieves can break in and steal. But store up treasures for yourselves in heaven.'

Matthew 6:19–20

Comment   As Christians our trust should not be in money and material things but in God and his loving care of us. If we place ourselves trustingly in the hands of God, who has made us, our hearts will be light and joyful.

Hymn and Prayer   'Give me joy in my heart', CH 84, FH I 78, FP 105, HON 78, NL 63, NO 70, SLW 4.

ALTERNATIVES

Hymns   'Do not worry', CH 63, FH I 33, FP 143, HON 61.
'Happy the man', CH 111, FH I 53, FP 86, HON 99.
'Lead us, heavenly Father, lead us', AM 311, CH 165, PL 112.

Prayers   See assembly 13 or 40 (alternative prayer).

31   The Christian Vocation

Hymn	'It's me, it's me, O Lord', CH 144, FH I 21, FP 113, HON 127.
Comment	Every day hundreds of people, throughout Great Britain, ring up the Samaritans for help because they are depressed or in trouble of some kind.
Reading	Chad Varah was an Anglican priest. In 1953 he buried a girl of 18 who had killed herself. The coroner, at her inquest, suggested that she might not have done this desperate act if someone had been around who would have listened to her troubles. Chad Varah decided to use his London church and a telephone to listen to people who were in despair. He put a small advertisement in the local paper, and during the first week he had 27 calls.

Soon he was listening and advising people 12 hours each day. There were so many people waiting in his outer office to see him that he asked some of his congregation to come and provide cups of tea for them. Then he found that often people who had come into the outer office in great distress had become different people by the time they reached him, and some did not even wait to see him because one of the helpers had befriended them. So he decided to train a group of his congregation so that they could be more helpful in the way they befriended the clients.

That is how the Samaritans were formed.

Patricia Curley |
| *Comment* | If Chad Varah had not gone to the inquest on the girl who had killed herself and heard the words of the coroner he might never have started that wonderful organisation which has saved so many lives – the Samaritans. God spoke to him through that man. He was called to a special work. |
| *Scripture reading* | Luke 10:1–12 or *New World*, p.140. |

Comment   Jesus 'called' his friends to join him in his special work
and sent them out to preach the Good News.

Prayer   O Divine Master, grant that I may not so much seek
to be consoled, as to console,
to be understood, as to understand,
to be loved, as to love;
for it is in giving that we receive,
it is in pardoning that we are pardoned,
and it is in dying that we are born to
eternal life.

St Francis of Assisi

Hymn   'Forth in thy name, O Lord, I go', AM 336, CH 79, NL
109, PL 87.

ALTERNATIVES

Hymns   'Who would true valour see', AM 293, NL 112, NO 61.
'Sing my soul', CH 278, FH I 62, FP 31.
'All that I am', CH 11, FH I 49, FP 61.

Prayers   See assembly 21 or 7 (alternative prayer).

32   Respect for Authority

Hymn   'Let all that is within me', CH 167, FH I 15, FP 159, HON
148, SLW 20.

Comment   Respect for authority, which is the theme of this
assembly, can be founded on fear or love.

Reading   A government surveyor one day brought his theodolite
along to a farm, called on the farmer and asked permission to set it up in a field nearby to take readings. Seeing
the farmer's unwillingness to let him enter the field, he
produced his papers and explained that he had government authority for entering the field and could, on
the same authority, go anywhere in the country to take
necessary readings. Reluctantly the farmer opened the
barred gate and allowed him to enter and set up his

survey table, but went to the other end of the field and let in the fiercest of his bulls. The surveyor was greatly alarmed at seeing the bull approach, and the farmer from the other side of the gate shouted to him 'Show him your credentials: show him your authority'.

Anon.

Comment   We can be obedient because we fear or because we love and respect the person who asks for something of us.

Scripture reading   John 15:9–17 or *New World*, p.396.

Prayer   Lord, I know that the best way to respect your commandments is to think of them as coming from you as loving requests. One of the best ways I can show love for you is by loving other people.

   Sometimes this is easy – when I'm with people I like. Please help me when loving is hard, when people are unkind, when they don't understand – when I just don't like them. Teach me to love as you loved; help me to keep your commandments, for in that way I show love to you.

Hymn   'Love is his word', CH 185, FH I 66, FP 107, HON 166, PL 75.

ALTERNATIVES

Hymns   'The Lord's my shepherd', CH 312, HON 267, NL 92, PL 115, SLW 102.
   'When I needed a neighbour', CH 353, FH I 41, NL 123, NO 13, PL 298.
   'Immortal, invisible', AM 372, CH 134, HON 121, NL 77.

Prayers   See assembly 25 or 31.

33   Forgiveness

Hymn   'God is love: his the care', CH 97, FP 43, HON 87, NL 132, NO 34, PL 276.

Reading 1   Rabbi Leo Baeck, a German scholar who took on the leadership of German Jews in Hitler's time, is a fine example of forgiveness. He was five times arrested, and finally sent to a concentration camp, where he served on the convicts' committee of management. On the very day he was to have been shot, the Russian troops arrived. Baeck could have escaped at once, but stayed behind to argue with the Russians, to persuade them to spare the lives of the German camp guards. The Russians decided that the camp guards should be handed over to the inmates. Baeck then argued with the inmates and managed to persuade them not to take the vengeance that they were thirsting for. Later on he went to the U.S.A. and worked hard for the Council of Christians and Jews. He died in 1956, aged 80.

Anon.

Reading 2   The Duke of Wellington was about to pronounce the death sentence on a confirmed deserter. Deeply moved, the great general said, 'I am extremely sorry to pass this severe sentence, but we have tried everything, and all the discipline and penalties have failed to improve this man who is otherwise a brave and good soldier'.

Then he gave the man's comrades an opportunity to speak for him. 'Please, your Excellency', said one of them, 'there is one thing you have never tried. You have not tried forgiving him.' The general forgave him and it worked; the soldier never again deserted and ever after showed his gratitude to the Iron Duke.

Anon.

Comment   We all do things that, from time to time, need forgiving. We must be prepared to say sorry and to ask forgiveness – when we know we have done wrong. And offer forgiveness to others, when they have hurt us.

Scripture reading   Matthew 18:21–22 or *New World*, p.64.

Prayer   Dear God, I find it so hard to forgive those who are unkind to me, or who blame me for things which are not my fault. I go on bearing a grudge against them and even when they try to make it up I feel bitter and hard.

I know this is wrong. When Peter asked Jesus how many times he ought to forgive someone who had wronged him, Jesus said he must go on and on forgiving. Jesus even prayed for forgiveness for those who crucified him. Please help me to be more like him and be willing to forgive.

Nancy Martin

Hymn   'Make me a channel', CH 189, FH I 35, FP 108, HON 167, SLW 97.

ALTERNATIVES

Hymns   'It's me, it's me, O Lord', CH 144, FH I 21, FP 113, HON 127.
'Walk with me, oh my Lord', CH 340, FH II 2, FP 191, HON 292.
'O sinner man', CH 229, FH I 22.

Prayers   See assembly 3 or 44.

34   Temptation

Comment   Let us think for a moment of the sea. Some of you might be imagining a clear blue peaceful sea as you see it on your summer holiday; some may be remembering winter storms shown on TV news when coastal towns were battered and ships were in distress.

Scripture reading   Mark 4:35–41 or *New World*, p.13.

Comment   The friends of Jesus were terrified of the stormy sea; they were tempted to doubt – they lacked faith.

Reading   *Light shining out of Darkness*
God moves in a mysterious way
   His wonders to perform;
He plants his footsteps in the sea,
   And rides upon the storm.

Deep in unfathomable mines
    Of never-failing skill
He treasures up his bright designs,
    And works his sovereign will.

Ye fearful saints fresh courage take;
    The clouds ye so much dread
Are big with mercy, and shall break
    In blessings on your head.

Judge not the Lord by feeble sense,
    But trust him for his grace;
Behind a frowning providence
    He hides a smiling face.

His purposes will ripen fast
    Unfolding every hour;
The bud may have a bitter taste,
    But sweet will be the flower.

Blind unbelief is sure to err,
    And scan his work in vain;
God is his own interpreter,
    And he will make it plain.

William Cowper

Prayer

Lord Jesus, I have watched the sea when I have been to
the coast on holiday.
    Even in summer, the waves pound the beach and hiss
over the shingle.
    As if they were living, angry things.

I have watched the sea on the television news in winter
When great breakers have pounded the promenades
And tossed cars about as if with a giant hand.

I'm always a bit afraid of the sea, Lord,
Even in its summer moods.

Yet you could stand erect in a heaving boat
And command the tumbling waves to be still.
No wonder your disciples were amazed.
What courage you showed!

Please share that courage with me, Lord Jesus.

Great waves of temptation beat against the shores of my
heart
Help me to still the storm,
And bring me to the safe harbour of your peace.

Mary Drewery

(This prayer is also used at assembly 29)

Hymn   'My God loves me', CH 205, FH II 24, FP 197, HON 176.

ALTERNATIVES

Hymn   'Lord for tomorrow', CH 178, HON 156, PL 168.
'Walk with me, oh my Lord', CH 340, FH II 2, FP 191,
HON 292.
'Make me a channel', CH 189, FH I 35, FP 108, HON 167,
SLW 97.

Prayers   O Lord God, grant us always, whatever the world may
say, to content ourselves with what thou wilt say, and to
care only for thine approval, which will outweigh all
words; for Jesus Christ's sake. Amen.

General Gordon

See also assembly 3 or 24.

35   God with Us

Hymn   'Immortal, invisible, God only wise', AM 372, CH 134,
HON 121, NL 77.

Comment   It's easy to think of God as a fearful, far-away figure
who is not very interested in us. Too distant and remote
to be approached. This is what Jimmy Savile says about
fearing God.

Reading   God does not frighten me in the way that a horror film
does. God, however, does fill me with complete
respect.
You see, I am in the business of kidding people in a
very light-hearted way. I am rather like a magician who

will, by sleight of hand, deceive you. Or I am like a
clown, who by purposeful and very careful thought-out
blunderings makes you laugh. I am both the deceiver –
in the best sense, I hope – and a blunderer with words. I
think that I can turn most people on when I start with
my light-hearted words and such like. But I have to be
very careful because if I ever slipped up and thought I
could deceive God, then my whole world would be
worth nothing. I have no need to be afraid of God; you
have no need to be afraid of God. Neither of us need be
afraid of anything. But God has my complete respect.
You see God is impossible to kid.

As a matter of fact, I actually enjoy God because I
have come to terms with that fact – that God cannot be
kidded.

Jimmy Savile

Comment   God can't be kidded – it means it's not a matter of
fearing God but respecting him, for he is so close to us
that he knows us inside out.

Scripture   Psalm 139:1–14 or *Winding Quest*, p.402.
reading

Prayer   Christ be with me,
   Christ within me,
Christ behind me,
   Christ before me,
Christ beside me,
   Christ to win me,
Christ to comfort and restore me,
Christ beneath me,
   Christ above me,
Christ in quiet and
   Christ in danger,
Christ in hearts of all that love me,
Christ in mouth of friend and stranger.

St Patrick

Hymn   'Walk with me, oh my Lord', CH 340, FH II 2, FP 191,
HON 292.

ALTERNATIVES

Hymns   'He's got the whole world', CH 117, FH I 29, FP 58, NO 86.

'It's me, it's me, O Lord', CH 144, FH I 21, FP 113, HON 127.

Prayers   See assembly 4 or 9 (alternative prayer).

36   Creation

Hymn   'Morning has broken', CH 196, FH I 73, FP 196, HON 171, NL 79, SLW 9.

Comment   'Like the first morning', the hymn said. Do we appreciate the beauty of the world God has created for us, when on the very first morning of the world's existence God started his work of creation?

Reading 1   A little girl who lived in a remote part of the country was receiving her first Bible instruction at the hands of her elderly grandmother, and the old lady was reading the child the story of the creation. After the story had been finished the little girl seemed lost in thought.

'Well, dear', said the grandmother, 'What do you think of it?'

'Oh, I love it. It's so exciting', exclaimed the young-ster. 'You never know what God is going to do next!'

Anon.

Comment   The little girl was quite right – you never know what God is going to do next. Each day his work of creation continues – with the birth of every new baby, the opening of each fragile flower, the invention of new computers and the discovery of medical techniques and cures. God's work of creation continues each day.

Reading 2   In a little church in the far South of Ireland, every window but one is of stained glass, representing Christ and his saints.

Through the one window which is plain glass may be seen a breath-taking view: a lake of deepest blue, studded with green islets, and backed by range after range of purple hills. Under the window is the inscription: 'The heavens declare the glory of God, and the firmament showeth his handiwork'.

Robert Gibbings

Comment Let us pause in silence to think of God's great power. That power which can create galaxies in outer space and tiny daisies in our fields.

Prayer O God, we thank thee for this earth, our home; for the wide sky and the blessed sun, for the salt sea and the running water, for the everlasting hills and the never-resting winds, for trees and the common grass underfoot. We thank thee for our senses by which we hear the songs of birds, and see the splendour of the summer fields, and taste of the autumn fruits, and rejoice in the feel of the snow, and smell the breath of the spring. Grant us a heart wide open to all this beauty and save our souls from being so blind that we pass unseeing when even the common thornbush is aflame with thy glory; O God, our Creator, who livest and reignest for ever and ever.

Walter Rauschenbusch

Hymn 'Now thank we all our God', AM 379, CH 211, HON 180, NL 55, NO 33, PL 93.

ALTERNATIVES

Hymns 'All things bright and beautiful', AM 442, CH 13, HON 18.
'O Lord my God', CH 227, FH II 27, FP 8, HON 202.
'All creatures of our God and King', AM 172, CH 4, HON 6, NL 43, NO 9, PL 261.

Prayers For eyes whereby I clearly see
The many lovely things there be;
For lungs to breathe the morning air,
For nose to smell its fragrance rare;
For tongue to taste the fruits that grow,
For birds that sing and flowers that blow;

For limbs to climb, and swing, and run,
For skin to feel the cheerful sun;
For sun and moon and stars in heaven,
Whose gracious light is freely given;
The river where the green weed floats,
And where I sail my little boats;
The sea, where I can bathe and play,
The sands where I can race all day;
The pigeons wheeling in the sun,
Who fly more quickly than I run;
The winds that sing as they rush by,
The clouds that race across the sky;
The shelter of the shady woods,
Where I may spend my lonely moods;
The gabled house that is my home,
The garden where I love to roam,
And bless my parents, every day,
Though they be very far away,
Take thou my thanks, O God above,
For all these tokens of thy love.
And when I am a man do thou
Make me as grateful then as now.

Richard Molesworth Dennis (who died in the
1914–1918 war)

See also assembly 51.

37   Supreme Being

Hymn	'Immortal, invisible', AM 372, CH 134, HON 121, NL 77.
Comment	This hymn emphasises the infinite, awe-inspiring power and splendour of God; but this is the same God that Jesus called 'Abba', which we would translate as 'Daddy'.
Scripture reading	Luke 10:21–22 or *New World*, p.98, 5–6.
Comment	One of Jesus's most important tasks was to make this God better known, respected and loved.

Reading

I offer you
Every flower that ever grew,
Every bird that ever flew,
Every wind that ever blew.
  Good God!

Every thunder rolling
Every church bell tolling,
Every leaf and sod.
  We praise you!

I offer you
Every wave that ever moved,
Every heart that ever loved,
You, your Father's Well-Beloved.
  Dear Lord.

Every river dashing,
Every lightning flashing,
Like an angel's sword.
  We bless you!

I offer you
Every cloud that ever swept
O'er the skies, and broke and wept
In rain, and with the flowerets slept.
  My King!

Each communicant praying,
Every angel staying,
Before your throne to sing.
  We adore you!

I offer you
Every flake of virgin snow,
Every spring of earth below,
Every human joy and woe,
  My love!

O Lord! And all your glorious
Self o'er death victorious,
Throned in heaven above.
  We glorify you!
         Ancient Irish prayer

Prayer	Supreme Lord and Father, we praise you for your creation, we adore you as your creatures, we bless you for all the good you shower on us, we glorify you for the death and resurrection of your Son, we love and thank you for your constant care of us. All this we express through Christ your Son. Amen.
Hymn	'O Lord my God', CH 227, FH II 27, FP 8, HON 202.

ALTERNATIVES

Hymns	'Let all that is within me', CH 167, FH I 15, FP 159, HON 148, SLW 20. 'All creatures of our God and King', AM 172, CH 4, HON 6, NL 43, NO 9, PL 261. 'Now thank we all our God', AM 379, CH 211, HON 180, NL 55, NO 33, PL 93.
Prayers	See assembly 51 or 36 (either prayer).

38   Worship

Hymn	'All people that on earth do dwell', AM 166, CH 10, HON 14, NL 44, PL 11.
Comment	This assembly has as its theme 'worship', the very thing that we try to do each time we gather here for prayers. The hymn we have just sung says, 'his praise forth tell', which means 'let's give a lot of praise and thanks to God'. And that is what worship is.
Reading 1	It is a law of man's nature, written into his very essence, and just as much a part of him as the desire to build houses and cultivate the land and marry and have children and read books and sing songs, that he should want to stand together with other men in order to acknowledge their common dependence on God, their Father and Creator. Thomas Merton

Reading 2   God is the supreme artist. He loves to have things beautiful. Look at the sunset and flowers and the snow-capped mountains and the stars. They are beautiful because they come from God. God loves to have things beautiful in church, too. And the same goes for church courtesies. To show our reverence for the cross on which he died for us, and for the Sacrament in which he comes to our hearts, is just to be polite to God. This is not required, but it is the part of Christian good breeding. It has the importance that courtesy has the world over.

John S. Baldwin

Comment   Saying 'thank you' to God is one way of praising and worshipping him, for by our gratitude for what he has done for us we are showing how much we depend on him and love him.

Prayer   O God, thank you for making me as I am.
Thank you for health and strength;
    For eyes to see;
    For ears to hear;
    For hands to work;
    For feet to walk and run.
For a mind to think;
For a memory to remember;
For a heart to love.
Thank you for
    Parents who are kind to me;
    Friends who are true to me;
    Teachers who are patient with me.
Thank you for this wonderful life. Help me to try to deserve all your gifts a little more.
This I ask for Jesus' sake. Amen.

William Barclay

Hymn   'Praise we our God with joy', CH 266, HON 228, PL 94.

ALTERNATIVES

Hymns   'Praise to the Lord', AM 382, CH 264, HON 226, NL 61, PL 14, SLW 11.
'Praise my soul', AM 365, CH 260, HON 223, NL 58, PL 95.

'Give me joy in my heart', CH 84, FH I 78, FP 105, HON 78, NL 63, NO 70, SLW 4.

Prayers O God, who hast made this great world, the sun and the moon and the stars; we thank thee for this wonderful earth, filled with all that we need for life. Teach us how to discover what is good and useful for everyone. Bless what men invent and use so that there is enough for everyone's need.

R.S. Macnicol

See also assembly 36.

39   Prayer

Hymn 'Oh, the love of my Lord', CH 231, FH I 79, FP 81, HON 195.

Comment There is a story of a priest (minister) who asked a little boy if he said his prayers each night. The boy said, Yes, he did. 'Do you say them in the morning?' the priest (minister) asked. 'No', said the lad, 'I ain't scared in the daytime!' Do we say prayers just because it's a habit or we're afraid not to – just in case something should happen if we don't? Prayer is talking to God and it requires an effort.

Reading 1 While journeying on horseback one day, St Benedict met a peasant walking along the road.

'You've got an easy job', said the peasant, 'Why don't I become a man of prayer? Then I too would be travelling on horseback.'

'You think praying is easy', replied the Saint. 'If you can say one "Our Father" without any distraction you can have this horse.'

'It's a bargain', said the surprised peasant.

Closing his eyes and folding his hands he began to say the Our Father aloud: 'Our Father, who art in heaven,

hallowed be Thy name, Thy Kingdom come . . .'
Suddenly he stopped and looked up.
'Shall I get the saddle and bridle too?'

Anon.

Comment   It's easy to be distracted while praying – prayer needs not only effort, to keep trying, but also love. We need to make a loving effort.

Reading 2   One day a mother noticed that her little girl was in her room a long time and she had said she was going to pray to Jesus. Finally when the little girl came out her mother asked her what she was doing in her room for such a long time when she had just gone in to pray. 'I was just telling Jesus that I love him and He was telling me that He loves me. And we were just loving each other.'

Anon.

Prayer   Dear Lord Jesus, teach us to be generous,
to serve you as you deserve,
to give and not to count the cost,
to fight and not to heed the wounds,
to toil and not to seek for rest,
to labour and ask for no reward
save that of knowing that we do your will. Amen.

St Ignatius Loyola

(This prayer is also used at assembly 21)

Hymn   'Give me joy in my heart', CH 84, FH I 78, FP 105, HON 78, NL 63, NO 70, SLW 4.

ALTERNATIVES

Hymns   'Praise we our God with joy', CH 266, HON 228, PL 94.
'All people that on earth do dwell', AM 166, CH 10, HON 14, NL 44, PL 11.
'Praise to the Lord', AM 382, CH 264, HON 226, NL 61, PL 14, SLW 11.

Prayer   See assembly 18.

40   Fasting and Penance

Hymn	'Walk with me', CH 340, FH II 2, FP 191, HON 292.
Comment	For the Christian, thoughts of fasting suggest the season of Lent – although it is not limited to a season.
Reading	The Saxons called March 'lencten monath' because in this month the days noticeably lengthen. As the chief part of the great fast, from Ash Wednesday to Easter, falls in March, it received the name Lencten-Faesten or Lent. The fast of 36 days was introduced in the fourth century, but it did not become fixed at 40 days until the early seventh century, thus corresponding with Our Lord's fast in the wilderness. *Anon.*
Comment	Our example and inspiration for the self-discipline of fasting comes from Jesus himself.
Scripture reading	Luke 4:1–13 (or *New World*, p.133 could be read in parts).
Prayer	Lord Jesus, we are thinking of you in the desert. We remember that for forty days and forty nights you were tempted there to disobey God's will. You know how often we are tempted to do wrong. Please show us how to overcome our temptations as you overcame your own. Help us to be strong-minded and teach us to banish wrong thoughts when they come. Make us true and brave and more like you every day. Brenda Holloway
Hymn	'All you who seek a comfort sure', AM 104, CH 15, PL 176.

ALTERNATIVES

Hymns	'The Lord's my shepherd', CH 312, HON 267, NL 92, PL 115, SLW 102. 'Lord for tomorrow', CH 178, HON 156, PL 168. 'One more step along the world', NO 35.

Prayers

Forgive me
When I ask you for too much –
When I forget to thank you for what I already have.
Forgive me, too, when I am selfish and demanding –
When I want to GET more than I want to GIVE.

Brother Kenneth and Sister Geraldine

See also assembly 18.

41 Care for Others

Comment

There is a beautiful English proverb that says 'He who plants trees loves others besides himself'.

Reading 1

Over 10,000 people in Provence, France, owe their homes and environment to a little-known peasant shepherd. Elezard Bouffier lived alone in 1910 in a barren region where there were very few trees. While tending his flock in the autumn, the shepherd would pick up each acorn that he saw. In the early spring, while watching the sheep, he would prod the earth with his staff and drop in a nut. He did this each year between 1910 and 1947. At his death, the barren countryside was covered by trees and teeming with wild life. It is now the pleasant site of a new housing development.

Anon.

Comment

It is so often the little things in life that count. Most of us hardly notice trees at all – but they can inspire poetry and thoughts of God.

Reading 2

I think that I shall never see
A poem lovely as a tree.

A tree whose hungry mouth is prest
Against the earth's sweet flowing breast;

A tree that looks at God all day,
And lifts her leafy arms to pray;

A tree that may in Summer wear
A nest of robins in her hair;

Upon whose bosom snow has lain;
Who intimately lives with rain.

Poems are made by fools like me,
But only God can make a tree.

Joyce Kilmer

Prayer   To pull up or destroy a tree, Lord, is to destroy something that you have created. It is to rob birds of a home, to take away shade, to make the landscape barren.

To plant a tree, or respect its growth, is to work with God the creator, to provide homes and shelter for birds, to share with generations not yet born a thing of beauty.

Lord, help us always to respect what you have made and work with you in the masterpiece of your Creation. Amen.

Hymn   'Praise my soul', AM 365, CH 260, HON 223, NL 58, PL 95.

ALTERNATIVES

Hymns   'Praise to the Lord', AM 382, CH 264, HON 226, NL 61, PL 14, SLW 11.
'All the nations', CH 12, FH I 81, FP 62, HON 17.
'Love is patient', FH IV 97.

Prayers   See assembly 36 (either prayer).

42   Inner Light

Comment   Have you ever been to a cathedral and admired the stained-glass windows? Chartres Cathedral in France has 175 magnificent windows. They were the first high-quality windows ever to be made and are still considered to be the best in the world. Their beauty and artistry can be appreciated only if you are inside when the sun pours through them or outside when bright lights shine out from within the cathedral.

Reading	People are like stained glass; they sparkle and shine when the sun is out, but when the darkness sets in, their true beauty is revealed only if there is light from within.

Elisabeth Kubler-Ross

Scripture readings	A	Matthew 6:22–23.
	B	Matthew 5:14–16.

Comment	After hearing the words about the light within us, let us hear our first reading again, and think more deeply on its meaning.
Reading	Repeat of reading above.
Prayer	Come Holy Spirit, light up our minds with your fire; destroy the darkness of selfishness that lurks within us. May we be so aglow with your love that people may see the good we do and give glory to the Father. We ask this through Christ, the light of the world. Amen.
Hymn	'Colours of day', CH 45, FH II 1, FP 9, HON 42.

ALTERNATIVES

Hymns	'Make me a channel', CH 189, FH I 35, FP 108, HON 167, SLW 97. 'Holy Spirit, Lord of light', CH 124, HON 109, PL 216. 'Holy Spirit of fire', CH 125, FH II 7, FP 90.
Prayers	See assembly 27 or 25.

43   Judgement

Hymn	'Lord for tomorrow', CH 178, HON 156, PL 168.
Reading	The Irish have a story of an Irishman who appeared before St Peter expecting admission, and when his ledger showed pages and pages of heavy debit entries, said that the books had been badly kept, for he knew he had once given twopence to a beggar. St Peter, after much flipping over of pages, found it so indeed; but

was twopence sufficient to outweigh all else? Then the Irishman said he had a friend called Patrick. If they would have the common politeness to call him he would make it all right. St Patrick was summoned, looked at the ledger, and he and St Peter exchanged doubtful glances.

'What are we to do with this countryman of yours?', asked St Peter. 'You see how it is.'

'Yes', said St Patrick, 'I see how it is. Give him back his twopence!'

Anon.

Comment
The hymn we sang reminded us that it's what we do today that matters; it is no good promising about tomorrow, if we make no effort today. The reading, in a humorous way, draws our attention to the fact that we will be judged on what we have done.

Scripture reading
Matthew 25:31–46 or *New World*, p.100.

Prayer
Lift up our hearts, O Christ, above the false show of things, above laziness and fear, above selfishness and covetousness, above custom and fashion, up to the everlasting Truth that thou art; that so we may live joyfully and freely, in the faith that thou art our King and our Saviour, our Example and our Judge, and that, as long as we are loyal to thee, all will be well with us in this world and in all worlds to come. Amen.

Hymn
'When I needed a neighbour', CH 353, FH I 41, NL 123, NO 13, PL 298.

ALTERNATIVES

Hymns
'Whatsoever you do', CH 352, FH I 71, FP 180, HON 298.
'God is love', CH 97, FP 43, HON 87, NL 132, NO 34, PL 276.

Prayers
See assembly 4, 44 or 40 (alternative prayer).

44   **Everlasting Life**

Hymn	'Lord of the dance', CH 131, FH I 68, NL 28, NO 54, PL 92.
Comment	'I am the life that will never, never die', says the hymn we have just sung – the words of Jesus. 'I'll live in you if you'll live in me.' That's a promise Jesus has made us. Listen to what some famous people have said about heaven.
Readings	A Confucius said, 'Heaven means to be one with God'.
	B Thomas Hardy said, 'The main object of religion is not to get a man into heaven, but to get heaven into him'.
	C Joseph Addison said, 'Heaven is not to be looked upon only as a reward, but as the natural effect of a good life'.
	D Dante said, 'If you insist on having your own way, you will get it. Hell is the enjoyment of your own way forever. If you really want God's way with you, you will get it in heaven'.
Scripture reading	John 14:1–4 or *New World*, p.394.
Prayer	All that we ought to have thought and have not thought, All that we ought to have said and have not said, All that we ought to have done and have not done, All that we ought not to have thought and yet have thought, All that we ought not to have spoken and yet have spoken, All that we ought not to have done and yet have done, For these words and works pray we, O God, For forgiveness, And repent with penance.

The Zendavesta, ascribed to Zoroaster, about 700 BC.

Hymn	'Morning has broken', CH 196, FH I 73, FP 196, HON 171, NL 79, SLW 9.

ALTERNATIVES

Hymns	'Make me a channel', CH 189, FH I 35, FP 108, HON 167, SLW 97.
	'Forth in thy name', AM 336, CH 79, NL 109, PL 87.
	'Walk with me', CH 340, FH II 2, FP 191, HON 292.
Prayers	See assembly 27 or 43.

45   Happiness

Hymn	'Happy the man', CH 111, FH I 53, FP 86, HON 99.
Comment	Happiness is what you and I and every human person seeks and longs for.
Reading	There was a medieval king who regularly used the advice of a wise man. This sage was summoned to the king's presence. The monarch asked him how to get rid of his anxiety and depression of spirits, how he might be really happy, for he was sick in body and mind. The sage replied, 'There is but one cure for the king. Your Majesty must sleep one night in the shirt of a happy man.'
	Messengers were despatched throughout the realm to search for a man who was truly happy. But everyone who was approached had some cause for misery, something that robbed them of true and complete happiness. At last they found a man – a poor beggar – who sat smiling by the roadside and, when they asked him if he was really happy and had no sorrows, he confessed that he was a truly happy man. Then they told him what they wanted. The king must sleep one night in the shirt of a happy man, and had given them a large sum of money to procure such a shirt. Would he sell them his shirt that the king might wear it? The beggar burst into uncontrollable laughter and replied, 'I am sorry I can-

not oblige the king. I haven't a shirt on my back.'

Anon.

Comment Often people are unhappy because they want to be what they are not, they haven't learnt to accept themselves as they are – they want to live in an unreal world, a dream world, a world of their fantasies.

Scripture reading Matthew 5:1–10 or *New World*, p.102.

Prayer Father Almighty, you made us to be happy, to be one with you; but when sin entered the world that happiness was frustrated. We all long to be happy, but it is all too easy to look for it in the wrong places. Please help each of us to seek happiness through kindness and service to others. We ask this through Christ your Son. Amen.

Hymn 'Give me joy in my heart', CH 84, FH I 78, FP 105, HON 78, NL 63, NO 70, SLW 4.

ALTERNATIVES

Hymns 'Let all that is within me', CH 167, FH I 15, FP 159, HON 148, SLW 20.
'Lord of all hopefulness', CH 181, HON 162, NL 54, NO 39, PL 288, SLW 44.
'Love divine, all loves excelling', AM 205, CH 184, HON 165, PL 113.

Prayers See assembly 35 or 51.

46 Family

Hymn 'The family of man', NL 113, NO 10.

Comment The opening song reminds us that we all belong to the family of the human race; in a sense we are brothers and sisters of one another. But, of course, we also belong to our own personal family. Little things make up family life.

Reading 1   A glimpse of a pram through the window,
A whistle from Auntie Bee;
A rat-tat at the letter box,
And the cousins are here for tea.
Marion is bald, as babies are,
Peter has short red hair;
Mother takes charge of Marion,
But Peter falls to my share.

Now the bricks go back to the cupboard,
And we settle down to our teas,
And I'll tell you something peculiar:
Peter likes jam with his cheese;
But before the meal's half over
He squirms for his mother's lap
Or crawls round the legs of the table,
Till he gets what he wants – a good slap.

                                                    J. Walsh

Comment   We don't just *belong* to a family, we have duties and
responsibilities in our family life. We are each in one
another's care.

Reading 2   A well-timed bite by a four-year-old girl, with a good
sense of smell, saved her family from gas poisoning.
        A peculiar odour awakened the child at 3 o'clock one
morning and she hurried to her father's room to tell
him.
        When a vigorous shake failed to disturb his peaceful
slumber, she bit him on the arm. That did the trick.
        The police discovered that the strange smell was
caused by monoxide fumes from the family car which
had been left running in the adjoining garage.
        The parents and all three children were in good
condition after being administered a dose of oxygen.

                                                    Anon

Prayer   Let us give thanks to God for our homes and families
and pray that we may grow in appreciation of all that we
have been given in love and material blessings over the
years. May we be kept from treating our homes as
lodging houses and from showing insufficient concern

for our parents. As we thank God for our homes we pray for all the homeless throughout the world.

We remember the homeless in this country.

We think of all the refugees – keep their distress in our minds – it is so easy for 'refugee' to become just a word to us. We make this prayer in the name of Jesus who lived in a family in Nazareth.

K.A. Clegg

Hymn 'We are one in the Spirit', CH 342, FH I 46, HON 294, PL 296.

ALTERNATIVES

Hymns 'Love is something if you give it away', NL 134, NO 14.
'Make me a channel', CH 189, FH I 35, FP 108, HON 167, SLW 97.
'Thank you,' CH 298, FH I 95, HON 257, PL 275.

Prayers See assembly 31 or 1 (alternative prayer).

---

47   God has no Favourites

Hymn 'Moses I know you're the man', CH 197, FH I 98, HON 172.

Comment We are God's people, members of his family. In his family God has no favourites – he doesn't prefer people of one colour to people of another, and he's not interested in which country we live, or whether we are rich or poor.

Scripture reading Romans 2:6–11 or *New World*, p.297.

Comment God does not see the colour of our skin, or whether we are popular with others or not. God has no enemies and no favourites.

Reading (This reading is taken from Ernest Gordon's account of life in a Japanese prison camp during the Second World

War. What you are about to hear takes place towards the end of the prisoners' captivity, after they had been brutally treated by their Japanese captors.)

Farther on, we were shunted on to a siding for a lengthy stay. We found ourselves on the same track with several carloads of Japanese wounded. They were on their own and without medical care. No longer fit for action, they had been packed into railway trucks which were being returned to Bangkok. Whenever one of them died en route, he was thrown off into the jungle. The ones who survived to reach Bangkok would presumably receive some form of medical treatment there. But they were given none on the way. They were in a shocking state; I have never seen men filthier. Their uniforms were encrusted with mud, blood and excrement. Their wounds, sorely inflamed and full of pus, crawled with maggots. . . . Without a word most of the officers in my section unbuckled their packs, took out part of their ration and a rag or two, and with water canteens in their hands went over to the Japanese train to help them. Our guards tried to prevent us, bawling, 'No goodka! No goodka!' But we ignored them and knelt by the side of the enemy to give them food and water, to clean and bind their wounds, to smile and say a kind word. Grateful cries of 'Aragatto' (thank you) followed us when we left. An allied officer from another section of the train had been taking it all in. 'What bloody fools you all are!' he said to me. 'Don't you realise that those are the enemy?'

Ernest Gordon

Prayer   Almighty God, we know that you love everyone and have no favourites. Help us to be like you, to treat everyone, especially those we find it difficult to get on with, with care and kindness. We ask you this through your Son, Jesus, who died for everyone regardless of their colour or creed. Amen.

Hymn   'Make me a channel', CH 189, FH I 35, FP 108, HON 167, SLW 97.

ALTERNATIVES

Hymns   'We are one in the Spirit', CH 342, FH I 46, HON 294, PL 296.
'The family of man', NL 113, NO 10.
'Whatsoever you do', CH 352, FH I 71, FP 180, HON 298.

Prayers   See assembly 6 or 3.

48   Refugees

Hymn   'When I needed a neighbour', CH 353, FH I 41, NL 123, NO 13, PL 298.

Comment   Whenever there's a war, there are people fleeing from the fighting area – refugees. When people are deprived of their freedom, they try to escape to where they can be free.

Reading   In a daring manoeuvre, ships of three nations combined to save a refugee family from Communist pursuers in busy shipping lanes in the Baltic Sea.

An East German police boat was bearing down with its machine guns on the little kayak whose tiny outboard motor had stalled. Ignoring the danger of collision, a Danish ferry captain swung his vessel sharply, putting it between pursuers and pursued.

The police boat began to swing around the Danish boat but then a Swedish ferry speedily moved in to block it again as passengers on both ships cheered.

Finally a West German freighter reached the terrified refugees, lowered a ladder and hauled them aboard.

The yearning for freedom, whether it is political, social, intellectual, economic, racial or religious, is embedded so deeply in every man that he will often risk life itself to achieve it.

Anon.

Comment For many years the Jewish people, God's chosen people, lived as exiles, or refugees, in a foreign land. They thanked God for his goodness, but longed to return home.

Prayer Teach us, O Lord, to hope in your Name, which is the source and fount of all creation. Open the eyes of our hearts to know you, who alone are Highest amid the highest, and ever abide Holy amidst the holy.

Deliver the afflicted, pity the lowly, raise the fallen reveal yourself to the needy, heal the sick, and bring home your wandering people.

Feed the hungry, ransom the captive, support the weak, comfort the faint-hearted.

Let all the nations of the earth know that you are God alone, that Jesus Christ is your child, and that we are your people and the sheep of your pasture.

To you, who alone can grant to us these and other yet more excellent benefits, we offer our praises through Jesus Christ, the High Priest and Guardian of our souls; through whom be glory and majesty to you now and for all generations and unto ages of ages. Amen.

Clement of Rome

Hymn 'God's Spirit is in my heart', CH 99, FH I 57, FP 35, HON 89, NL 116, SLW 93.

ALTERNATIVES

Hymns 'Whatsoever you do', CH 352, FH I 71, FP 180, HON 298. 'Show me the prison', NL 105. 'We shall overcome', CH 348, FH I 31, FP 163.

Prayers Lord Jesus, we remember how, when you were born there was no place in all the town of Bethlehem to lay a baby down. Take now into your loving care all homeless children everywhere. And we remember how, at Galilee, the waiting crowd as by a miracle was fed, on two small fishes and five loaves of bread. Lord Jesus listen to our prayer, feed hungry children everywhere.

Sally Cawley

See also assembly 6.

49   Gypsies

Hymn   'All people that on earth do dwell', AM 166, CH 10, HON 14, NL 44, PL 11.

Comment   The hymn we have just sung opens with the words, 'All people', and that would include one of the most disrespected groups in the country – the gypsies.

Reading 1   The village folk of Stephen's Green, Kent, are up in arms again over gypsies. Six of the estimated 7,000 travelling families in the country camped last Friday on the wide grass verge alongside the A25, on the west side of the station. The parish council summoned an emergency meeting last night to seek ways of moving the gypsies on and stopping their return. Councillor Carter's boldly proposed idea of seeking land for a permanent site for them was rejected out of hand. Mr Carter had tried to point out that the Caravan Site Act of Parliament encouraged the setting up of sites for the travelling families. So far less than 200 have been provided, which means that two out of every three families have no permanent pitch to use.

     Councillor Carter accused the parish council of acting in a very un-Christian fashion, as they sought ways to hound the gypsies from the area.

Anon.

Comment   The United Nations Charter of Human Rights declares 'All human beings are born free and equal in dignity and rights'. A Christian would put it this way –

Reading 2   We are no longer outsiders and foreigners in God's world; we are fellow-citizens with all the friends of Jesus everywhere and members of God's family.

Alan Dale

Prayer   We pray for those who feel isolated and neglected.

ALL   We are members of God's family and pray for them.

     We pray for the persecuted, the unwanted, the refugees.

ALL   We are members of God's family and pray for them.

           We pray for the minority groups throughout the world
           and especially for gypsies in this country.

ALL   We are members of God's family and pray for them.

Hymn   'We are one in the spirit', CH 342, FH I 46, HON 294, PL
           296.

ALTERNATIVES

Hymns   'When I needed a neighbour', CH 353, FH I 41, NL 123,
           NO 13, PL 298.
           'Whatsoever you do', CH 352, FH I 71, FP 180, HON 298.
           'Love is his word', CH 185, FH I 66, FP 107, HON 166, PL
           75.

Prayers See assembly 46 or 6.

50   The Hungry

Hymn   'Feed us now', CH 72, FH I 103.

Scripture   Mark 6:35–44 or *New World*, p.25.
reading

Comment   In that reading we heard how concerned Jesus was for
                    those who were hungry. Many organisations and indi-
                    viduals today work to relieve the undernourished.

Reading 1   Many years ago, during the Second World War, a
                    group of people in Oxford got together to send aid to
                    children starving in Greece. They called themselves the
                    Oxford Committee for Famine Relief and before long
                    they were known as Oxfam. Their work spread: from
                    Oxford to many other towns and cities; from helping
                    Greek children to any group in need. Thousands of
                    volunteers collected money through fund-raising
                    events, shops were opened to sell second-hand clothes
                    and every possible method of raising money was used

Oxfam became world-famous for its relief work.

Reading 2   It is difficult to select and talk of individuals who have helped feed the hungry, as Christ taught us to do, because so many have made great sacrifices that are known only to God. Two internationally known figures, from the world of pop music, stand out simply because they are both superstars and good christians.

Cliff Richard's commitment and support for TEAR fund has meant that that relief organisation has been able to give tremendous aid to the deprived. Jimmy Savile helps and supports many different funds and charitable organisations. On his own he has raised over 5 million pounds in the past few years; and he has every intention of carrying on for as long as the 'Good Lord' – as Jimmy calls him – gives him strength.

Anon.

Prayer   Lord Jesus, we remember how you were concerned for and fed a waiting crowd of people in Galilee. Bless and help all those organisations and individuals who show your concern for the hungry of our world. Help us too to do all we can to share your concern. Amen.

Hymn   'When I needed a neighbour', CH 353, FH I 41, NL 123, NO 13, PL 298.

ALTERNATIVES

Hymns   'Whatsoever you do', CH 352, FH I 71, FP 180, HON 298.
'Sing we the song of high revolt', NL 12.
'There is a world', CH 317, FH I 97, FP 137, HON 271, NL 106.

Prayers   See assembly 52 or 38 (alternative prayer).

51   Thanksgiving

Hymn   'Give me joy in my heart', CH 84, FH I 78, FP 105, HON 78, NL 63, NO 70, SLW 4.

Scripture reading   Luke 17:11–19 or *New World*, p.145.

Comment   Of the ten healed only one returned to say 'Thank you'. Jesus told us that we have much to learn from the simplicity of little children. Here are two stories from which we might learn.

Reading 1   Little Janie was being taught that it was the proper thing to do to write a 'thank you' letter to those persons who sent her gifts at Christmas. She seemed to do pretty well until it came to Aunt Martha's gift. Finally she finished her note which read: 'Thank you for your Christmas present. I always wanted a pin-cushion, although not very much.'

Anon.

Reading 2   The church nursery-school teacher had placed a lovely bouquet of daffodils on the table in the nursery room. When little Sandra came into the room she was fascinated by the flowers and said to her teacher, 'Aren't these pretty telephones God made? I think I'll call God up and say, "Thank you for the pretty flower".'

Anon.

Comment   Christians should have a 'thank you' attitude to life; always ready to thank God, for to say 'thank you' is another way of saying 'We love you'.

Prayer   For flowers that bloom about our feet,
Father, we thank thee,
For tender grass so fresh, so sweet,
Father, we thank thee.
For the song of bird and hum of bee,
For all things fair we hear or see,
Father in heaven, we thank thee.

For blue of stream and blue of sky
Father, we thank thee.
For pleasant shade of branches high,
Father, we thank thee.
For fragrant air and cooling breeze,
For the beauty of the blooming trees,
Father in heaven, we thank thee.

For this new morning with its light,
Father, we thank thee.
For rest and shelter of the night,
Father, we thank thee.
For health and food, for love and friends,
For everything thy goodness sends,
Father in heaven, we thank thee.

Ralph Waldo Emerson

Hymn   'Thank you', CH 298, FH I 95, HON 257, PL 275.

ALTERNATIVES

Hymns   'Now thank we all our God', AM 379, CH 211, HON 180, NL 55, NO 33, PL 93.
'Praise we our God with joy', CH 266, HON 228, PL94.
'Praise my soul the King of heaven', AM 365, CH 260, HON 223, NL 58, PL 95.

Prayers   See assembly 36 (either prayer).

52   Freedom

Hymn   'We shall overcome', CH 348, FH I 31, FP 163.

Reading   Thirteen East German refugees who fled to West Berlin said that the hours they spent in their escape tunnel were like 'eternity in a coffin'.

Among those who made their way through the 60-yard tunnel were a blind woman, a 70-year-old grandmother pulled along by a rope and two boys who were told to pretend they were playing hedgehogs.

The digging was all done with a spade by a 42-year-old handyman and a 20-year-old medical student. The tunnel, less than 2 feet high, extended from a four-room house without a cellar, under three rows of barbed wire, to a garden behind a shop in the French sector of the city.

The desperate effort made by people to regain freedom should teach us all a lesson that is so hard to learn but one that could save mankind so much suffering. Do whatever you can to bring about peace based on justice. Never forget that this big challenge starts with your prayers, words and deeds as much as it does with anyone else's.

Anon.

Prayer

O God, within whose sight
All men have equal rights
To worship thee,
Break every bar that holds
Thy flock in diverse folds;
Thy will from none withholds
Full liberty.

Lord, set thy churches free
From foolish rivalry;
Lord, set us free!
Let all past bitterness
Now and for ever cease,
And all our souls possess
Thy charity!

Lord, set the people free!
Let all men draw to thee
In unity!
Thy temple courts are wide,
Therein, let all abide
In peace, and side by side
Serve only thee!

God, grant us now thy peace!
Bid all dissensions cease!
God, send us peace!
Peace in true liberty,
Peace and fraternity,
God, send us peace!

John Oxenham

Hymn

'Forth in thy name, O Lord, I go', AM 336, CH 79, NL 109, PL 87.

ALTERNATIVES

Hymns   'When Israel was in Egypt's land', CH 354, FH I 19, FP 148, HON 300, NL 98.
'Peace, perfect peace', CH 257, FH I 2, FP 120, HON 220.

Prayers   See assembly 24 or 3.

53   Hope

Hymn   'Lord of all hopefulness', CH 181, HON 162, NL 54, NO 39, PL 288, SLW 44.

Comment   There is an old proverb that says 'While there's life there's hope'. Too often people get discouraged, when things get difficult, and just give up.

Reading 1   When Sir Walter Scott was a boy, he was considered a great dullard. His accustomed place in the schoolroom was the ignominious dunce's corner, with the high-pointed paper cap of shame on his head. When about 12 years old, he happened to be in a house where some famous literary guests were being entertained. Robert Burns, the Scottish poet, was standing admiring a picture under which was written the couplet of a stanza. He inquired concerning the author. None seemed to know. Timidly a boy crept up to his side, named the author, and quoted the rest of the poem. Burns was surprised and delighted. Laying his hand on the boy's head, he exclaimed, 'Ah, bairnie, ye will be a great man in Scotland some day'. From that day Walter Scott was a changed lad. One word of encouragement set him on the road to greatness.

                                        Anon.

Reading 2   Do you know the story of the two frogs that fell into a bucket of cream? They tried hard to get out by climbing up the side of the bucket. But each time they slipped back again.

    Finally one frog said: 'We'll never get out of here. I

give up.' So down he went and drowned. The other frog decided to keep trying. So again and again he tried to climb with his front legs and he kicked with his back legs. Suddenly he hit something hard. He turned to see what it was and discovered that all his kicking had churned up a lump of butter! He hopped on top of it and leaped out to safety.

Anon.

Comment   Trying to overcome discouragement is hope in action; we must always be confident of God's caring love; there is a glorious future – just around the corner.

Scripture reading   Romans 8:18–25 or *New World*, p.306.

Prayer   Lord, when things don't seem to be going very well, in fact, we are discouraged and fed up, help us to place all our confidence in you. Give us the patience we need to trust in your loving care, please give us the gift of hope. This we ask through Christ your Son. Amen.

Comment   Although things went very badly for Jesus on the last day of his life he never lost hope.

Hymn   'Lord of the dance', CH 131, FH I 68, NL 28, NO 54, PL 92.

ALTERNATIVES

Hymns   'There is a world', CH 317, FH I 97, FP 137, HON 271, NL 106.
'One more step along the world I go', NO 35.
'God is love', CH 97, FP 43, HON 87, NL 132, NO 34, PL 276.

54   Charity

Hymn   'Love is his word', CH 185, FH I 66, FP 107, HON 166, PL 75.

Comment   One of the most important things Jesus did was to tell us more about God. From Jesus we learnt that God doesn't have love, he *is* love. Those who try to know and love this God try to show his love to others.

Reading   Yes, the first woman I saw I myself picked up from the street. She had been half eaten by the rats and ants. I took her to the hospital but they could not do anything for her. They only took her in because I refused to move until they accepted her. From there I went to the municipality and I asked them to give me a place where I could bring these people because on the same day I had found other people dying in the streets. The health officer of the municipality took me to the temple, the Kali Temple, and showed me the dormashalah where the people used to rest after they had done their worship of Kali goddess. It was an empty building; he asked me if I would accept it. I was very happy to have that place for many reasons, but especially knowing that it was a centre of worship and devotion of the Hindus. Within 24 hours we had our patients there and we started the work of the home for the sick and dying who are destitutes. Since then we have picked up over 23,000 people from the streets of Calcutta of which about 50 per cent have died.

Mother Teresa

(This reading is also used at assembly 7)

Prayer

READER   If I have passed the highest examination in English, and speak like a newscaster, but have no warmth of love.

ALL   I am nothing.

READER   If I have learnt so much that my mind is like a computer, but have not an understanding of love.

ALL   I am nothing.

READER   If I am a person of great faith and ideals, but I have no time to spare for other people.

ALL   I am nothing.

READER   If I leave home, my family and friends and give myself to the work of the Church, but remain selfish and lacking in love, then I'm nothing.

ALL I am nothing.

READER This is what love is like . . . 1 Corinthians 13:4–7.

Hymn 'Bind us together Lord', FH IV 21, HON 33.

ALTERNATIVES

Hymns 'Make me a channel', CH 189, FH I 35, FP 108, HON 167, SLW 97.
'God is love', CH 97, FP 43, HON 87, NL 132, NO 34, PL 276.
'Love divine, all loves excelling', AM 205, CH 184, HON 165, PL 113.

Prayers See assembly 39 or 27.

55 Peace

Hymn 'Give me joy in my heart', CH 84, FH I 78, FP 105, HON 78, NL 63, NO 70, SLW 4.

Reading *Pax*

All that matters is to be one with the living God, to be a creature
in the house of God of life.

Like a cat asleep on a chair
at peace, in peace
and at one with the master of the house, with the mistress,
at home, at home in the house of the living,
sleeping on the hearth, and yawning before the fire.

Sleeping on the hearth of the living world,
yawning at home before the fire of life
feeling the presence of the living God
like a great reassurance
a deep calm in the heart

a presence
as of a master sitting at the board
in his own and greater being
in the house of life.

D.H. Lawrence

Comment   True peace is a gift from God.

Scripture   Reader A   'Behold I stand at the door and knock, if
readings   any man hears my voice and opens the door, I will
with prayer   come in to him and eat with him and he with me.'

Revelation 3:20

(Little pause after each short reading)

ALL   Come Lord, fill us with your peace.

B   'If a man loves me, he will keep my word, and my
Father will love him, and we will come to him and make
our home with him!'

John 14:23

ALL   Come Lord, fill us with your peace.

C   'Abide in me, and I in you. As the branch cannot
bear fruit by itself, unless it abides in the vine, neither
can you, unless you abide in me.'

John 15:4

ALL   Come Lord, fill us with your peace.

D   'That Christ may dwell in your hearts through
faith. . . . That you may be filled with all the fullness of
God.'

Ephesians 3:17 and 19

ALL   Come Lord, fill us with your peace.

Hymn   'Peace, perfect peace', CH 257, FH I 2, FP 120, HON 220.

ALTERNATIVES

Hymns   'Peace is flowing like a river', CH 254, FH II 31, FP 221,
HON 219, SLW 91.
'Flowers of peace', NL 128.
'To Christ, the prince of peace', AM 198, CH 333, HON
286, PL 182.

Prayers   Your beautiful world is being spoilt today, dear God, by our selfishness and greed. Instead of peace there is discord and war. Instead of love there is hatred and fear.

Help us, O Lord, to shut out of our individual lives all that is selfish and greedy, all hatred and bitterness. Help us to have love and forgiveness in our hearts; the desire to help others and to share the good things of life. Then, perhaps, if we learn to live generously and peaceably as individuals we shall become a generous and peaceful nation and other nations will follow our example.

See also assembly 52 or 1 (alternative prayer).

56   The Light of Faith

Hymn   'I sing a song to you, Lord', CH 141, FH II 44, FP 103, HON 126.

Comment   Faith is often compared to light.

Readings   A   Faith, like light, should always be simple, and unbending; while love, like warmth, should beam forth on every side.

Martin Luther

B   Belief is a truth held in the mind. Faith is a fire in the heart.

Joseph Newton

Prayer

READER   I believe in God the Father who from the darkness of nothing created light and this beautiful world in which we live.

ALL   I believe in God the Father, Creator of the Universe.

READER   I believe in his Son who is with us when we walk alone and in darkness.

ALL   I believe in God the Son, born to be the light of the world.

READER	I believe in the Spirit of light and love by whose power we are born again to be children of God.
ALL	I believe in the Holy Spirit who lights up our minds and warms our hearts.
Hymn	'Lead us, heavenly Father, lead us', AM 311, CH 165, PL 112.

ALTERNATIVES

Hymns	'Firmly I believe and truly', AM 186, CH 75, HON 70, PL 219. 'Colours of day', CH 45, FH II 1, FP 9, HON 42.
Prayers	See assembly 24 or 27.

57　Loneliness

Hymn	'Walk with me, oh my Lord', CH 340, FH II 2, FP 191, HON 292.
Comment	We all like to be on our own, from time to time. To be alone isn't the same as being lonely. You can be lonely in a crowd of people. Lots of people are lonely.
Reading	'Dear Daddy' – in her best handwriting eleven-year-old Jane wrote a letter to her make-believe father every week. She addressed the envelope to herself, and every week without fail she wrote back – 'Dear Jane'. For this shy youngster living in a local authority home two postage stamps and a dream father were the only cure she had for an affliction that is so pathetically easy to diagnose – loneliness. At this moment there are four million desperately lonely people in this country. Before someone like young Jane grows into a lonely Mrs X I know who rings up the telephone speaking clock for company, why don't we act? *Daily Express*

Comment	There's never a good reason for a Christian to be really lonely, because Jesus, our friend, is always with us.
Scripture readings	A John 14:21. B John 14:23. C John 15:4–7.
Prayer	Grant, O our God, that we may know thee, and rejoice in thee; and if in this life we cannot do those things fully, grant that we may at least progress in them from day to day, for Christ's sake.

St Anselm

Hymn	'I watch the sunrise', CH 145, FH II 100, FP 84, HON 128.

ALTERNATIVES

Hymns	'Lord of all hopefulness', CH 181, HON 162, NL 54, NO 39, PL 288, SLW 44. 'Make me a channel', CH 189, FH I 35, FP 108, HON 167, SLW 97.
Prayers	God of the busy daytime; God of the quiet night; Whose peace pervades the darkness And greets us with the light. Save with thy presence near us Whatever we may be, Thou, God, our great protector We love and worship thee.

John Oxenham

See also assembly 24 or 4.

58   Elderly People

Hymn	'Lord for tomorrow', CH 178, HON 156, PL 168.
Scripture readings	A Isaiah 46:4. B Psalm 92:14. C Psalm 90:12. D Ecclesiastes 5:20.

Comment	Old age is a time for wisdom, for maturity. An opportunity to rest from the hard work of a lifetime and grow closer to God.
Scripture reading	John 2:10.
Prayer	Dear Father, we pray for all old people. Help us to respect them as people who have lived through childhood and youth; most of them have had families and are now grandparents or great-grandparents. Help us to respect them as mature adults who have grown in wisdom with the passing of the years. Comfort those who are sick, tired or lonely. Make us to be always thoughtful and considerate when we meet them, for they are special in your eyes; we ask you this through Jesus your Son. Amen.
Hymn	'The Lord's my shepherd', CH 312, HON 267, NL 92, PL 115, SLW 102.

ALTERNATIVES

Hymns	'Lord of all hopefulness', CH 181, HON 162, NL 54, NO 39, PL 288, SLW 44. 'There is a world', CH 317, FH I 97, FP 137, HON 271, NL 106. 'God is love', CH 97, FP 43, HON 87, NL 132, NO 34, PL 276.
Prayers	See assembly 35 or 9 (alternative prayer).

59   Perseverance

Hymn	'Give me joy in my heart', CH 84, FH I 78, FP 105, HON 78, NL 63, NO 70, SLW 4.
Comment	The theme of this assembly is 'perseverance' – that is, keeping steadily on with something worthwhile that you are doing, no matter what the problems and difficulties. For example, to climb Everest for the first

time was 'worthwhile' but it required a lot of hard work and perseverance.

Reading   'Leaving Tenzing to belay me as best he could, I found my way into the crack, then kicking backwards with my crampons I sank their spikes deep into the frozen snow behind me and levered myself off the ground. Despite the considerable effort involved, my progress, although slow, was steady and as Tenzing played out the rope I inched my way upwards until I could finally reach the top of the rock and drag myself out of the crack on to a wide ledge.

For a few minutes I lay regaining my breath and for the first time really felt the fierce determination that nothing now could stop us reaching the top. I took a firm stance on the ledge and signalled to Tenzing to come on up. As I heaved hard on the rope Tenzing wriggled his way up the crack and finally collapsed exhausted at the top, like a giant fish when it has just been hauled from the sea after a terrible struggle. I was beginning to tire a little now. I had been cutting steps continuously for two hours and Tenzing too was moving very slowly. Our original zest had now quite gone and it was turning more into a grim struggle. I looked upwards to see a narrow snow ridge running up to a snowy summit. A few more whacks of the ice-axe in the firm snow and we stood on top.'

Sir Edmund Hillary in *The Ascent of Everest*
by Sir John Hunt

Comment   There are times when all our efforts to be good, to tell the truth, to pray and so on, seem pointless. It all seems too much effort. But God is always on hand to help.

Scripture   A   Psalm 42:11.
readings   B   Psalm 63:1.
　　　　　　　C   Mark 15:34.
　　　　　　　D   Psalm 40:1–2.

Comment   Let us conclude with the prayer of another explorer-adventurer, Sir Francis Drake, who must have often been tempted to give up.

Prayer	O Lord God, when you give grace to your servants to try to do some good work, grant that we may understand that is not the beginning but the persevering in trying until the end which gives you real glory.

Sir Francis Drake

Hymn	'Walk with me, oh my Lord', CH 340, FH II 2, FP 191, HON 292.

ALTERNATIVES

Hymns	'Christ be beside me', CH 41, FH II 13, FP 160, HON 39, PL 221a. 'Praise we our God with joy', CH 266, HON 228, PL 94. 'Breathe on me, breath of God', AM 236, CH 37, HON 34, NL 86, PL 6.
Prayers	Gracious God, remember us, we beseech thee, in our work this day. If it be thy will, give unto us a prosperous day. May all our work be well done. May we turn nothing out half done. May we glorify thee by honest good work; for the sake of him who completed his work for us, even Jesus Christ our Lord.

J.H. Fowett

See also assembly 39 or 9 (alternative prayer).

60   Quiet – Time for Reflection

Hymn	'Amazing Grace', CH 19, FH I 36, FP 73, HON 20, SLW 5.
Comment	God's help, his love and grace, can reach us at any time, anywhere; but we, like Jesus, should sometimes give ourselves the opportunity of quiet, so that God may have greater opportunity to touch our hearts and souls.
Scripture reading	
ALL	Be still and know that I am God (Psalm 46:10).
READER	Luke 4:1.

ALL	Be still, and know that I am God.
READER	1 Kings 19:11–12.
ALL	Be still, and know that I am God.
READER	Job 40:4–5; 42:5–6.
ALL	Be still and know that I am God.
READER	Luke 4:42.
ALL	Be still, and know that I am God.
Prayer	Lord, friendships do not grow if one friend does all the talking! Please help me not to forget that when I pray. There is a time for talking to you and a time for silence, to give you an opportunity to speak to me. May your gentle silence draw me closer to you. Amen.
Hymn	'Oh, the love of my Lord is the essence', CH 231, FH I 79, FP 81, HON 195.

ALTERNATIVES

Hymns	'Peace, perfect peace', CH 257, FH I 2, FP 120, HON 220. 'Morning has broken', CH 196, FH I 73, FP 196, HON 171, NL 79, SLW 9.
Prayer	See assembly 4.

ADDITIONAL READINGS

These readings may be used *ad lib.* according to the discretion of the
reader.

101

Who has seen the wind, neither you nor I,
But when the trees hang down their heads
The wind is passing by.

Who has seen the wind, neither I nor you,
But when the leaves hang trembling,
The wind is passing through.

Christina Rossetti

102

In years gone by, the court jester was an important member of the king's
household. By means of quips, he kept the king in good humour – and
entertained the members of the royal household.

Some writer tells us what he believes to be the best retort any court
jester gave. It was the retort given his sovereign, a dyspeptic dictator who
had the ancient 'power of life or death' over all his subjects, and it was
supposed to be legally impossible for the king to change any sentence he
set on the subject. Becoming irritated by his court jester, in a sudden rage
of wrath, the king sentenced his court jester to death. Then realising too
late his rash decree, the king said to the court jester:

'In consideration of your faithful services, I will permit you to select
the manner in which you prefer to die.' The court jester instantly
answered: 'I select to die of old age.'

Anon.

103

It is done. Once again the fire has penetrated the earth. Not with the
sudden crash of thunderbolt ringing the mountain tops does the Master
break down doors to enter his own home! Without earthquake or thun-
derclap, the flame has lit up the whole world from within. All things

individually and collectively are penetrated and flooded by it, from the inmost core of the tiniest atom to the mighty sweep of the most universal laws of being. So naturally has it flooded every element, every energy, every connecting link in the unity of our cosmos, that one might suppose the cosmos to have burst spontaneously into flame.

Pierre Teilhard de Chardin

104

A great American story-teller wrote about two young people who were very much in love. Christmas Eve was coming and they wanted to give presents to one another. But they were very poor and had no money for presents. So each one, without telling the other, decided to sell his or her most precious possession. The girl's most precious possession was her long golden hair and she went to a hairdresser and had it cut off. She sold it then to buy a lovely watch chain for her lover's watch. He, meanwhile, had gone to a jeweller and sold his watch to buy two beautiful combs for his beloved's hair. Then they made their gifts. There were tears at first, and then laughter. There was no hair for the combs and no watch for the watch chain. But there was something more precious and that was their self-sacrificing love for one another.

Anon.

105

There is a huge statue of Christ holding a Cross standing on the Andes, between the countries of Argentine and Chile. The story of that statue is worth knowing. Once Argentine and Chile were about to go to war with one another. They were quarrelling over some land which each said belonged to them. So both countries started to prepare for war. Then on Easter Sunday, bishops in Argentine and Chile began to urge peace. They went round their countries crying out for peace in the name of Christ. The people did not want war and in the end they made their governments talk peace with one another, instead of war. The big guns, instead of being used for fighting, were melted down and made into the great big bronze statue of Christ. It now stands on the mountain between the two countries. Written on it are the words 'These mountains shall fall and crumble to dust before the people of Chile and Argentine shall forget their solemn covenant sworn at the feet of Christ.'

Maurice Nassan

106

Not merely in the words you say, not only in the
 deeds confessed,
But in the most unconscious way is Christ
 expressed.
Is it a very saintly smile? A holy light upon your
 brow?
Oh no! I felt his presence while you laughed just
 now.
For me, 'twas not the truth you taught, to you so
 clear, to me so dim;
But when you came, you straightway brought a sense
 of him.
So from your life he beckons me, and from your
 heart his love is shed.
Till I lose sight of you, and see Christ instead.

Anon.

107

Little Jesus, Lord of all,
Cradled in the cattle stall,
Swaddled safe, content to lay
Warm and wanted on the hay;

Mary with maternal joy
Smiles upon her baby boy
Sleeping, sated, laid to rest
From the fulness of her breast.

Anxious Joseph making sure
All is well and all secure,
His the ward and watch to keep,
Bids the maiden mother sleep.

Ass and Ox, with eyes intent,
Gaze on them in wonderment,
Careful lest their cramped tread
Stir the infant in his bed.

All is quiet, all is peace;
Hush, you world, your quarrels cease.
Watch with Joseph, vigil keeping,
For the Son of God is sleeping.

Killian Twell, OFM

108

A man went to stay with a friend in Cornwall, in a part where there were a large number of deep holes in the ground. These were disused mine shafts, some of which had no rails round them. He went for a walk one day and got lost. Darkness came and he realised that he was near these holes and it was dangerous to walk in the dark. But it was too cold to sit down and wait till morning so he walked on with great care. In spite of this, his feet slipped and he started to slide down a mine-shaft. He managed to grasp a rock that was sticking out of the side of the shaft. There he hung, terrified, with his feet dangling. He managed to hang on for about twenty minutes, but the agony in his arms got so great that he knew he would soon have to let go and plunge to his death. He was about to let go when he saw, to his immense relief, a little light in the distance which began to grow greater and he knew that help was coming. He shouted loud with all the energy he had left. When the rescuers arrived and shone their light down on him, the first thing they saw was that his feet were dangling within a foot of solid earth. This mine-shaft had been filled in! All his agony and fears had been for nothing.

Maurice Nassan

109

The cell was a concrete box too narrow to sit down. One could only bend one's knees a little, so that they were thrust up against the door, and the position becomes so agonising that it is hard not to cry out. To pray in such circumstances is not easy, but it is a great and sweet solace if one can do so, and one must try with all one's strength to love more, not less. I had to struggle not to sink below the level of love and fall back into the realm of hatred, anger and revenge; to love Romulus Luca (the prison guard) not for a moment but continuously. I had to drive my soul to do this as one may push a vehicle with locked brakes. It was now that I came

to understand Luca, his blindness and narrow hatred, his reactions
which were like those of a dog rendered savage by being chained too long,
or of a slave put in charge of slaves, with no freedom except to torment
them. And then my thoughts went to those, whom it was natural and easy
to love. I found that now I loved them differently, now that I had learnt to
love Luca. . . . And it was in that cell, my legs sticky with filth, that I at
last came to understand the divinity of Jesus Christ, the most divine of all
men, the one who had most deeply and intensely loved, and who had
conceived the parable of the lost sheep.

Petru Dumitriu

110

'I do not know so much the situation in the West because I have been
away for such a long time – forty years. But now more and more there's
this. Lenten raising of money to help the poorest. It's growing, and
people are beginning to be more and more conscious that there are in the
world people who are hungry and who are naked and who are sick and
who have no shelter. And the rich want to share the hardship in some way,
just a little bit sometimes; the difficulty is that they don't give until it
hurts. The new generation, especially the children, are understanding
better. The children in England are making sacrifices to give a slice of
bread to our children and the children of Denmark are making sacrifices
to give a glass of milk to our children daily, and the children of Germany
are making sacrifices to give one multi-vitamin daily to a child. These are
the ways to greater love. These children when they grow up, they will
have faith and love and a desire to serve and to give more!'

Mother Teresa talking to Malcolm Muggeridge

111

Poverty is the moment in the world
When lilies and children
And all the things that matter,
Don't.
It is the moment when only bread
Is beautiful
Because it means another hour or two

Of living,
With only the hope that hope
is round the corner,
No idea or solution
From a perfect flower,
Only live from day to day,
Avoiding death.
Don't give a lily to a man like that.
If he is hungry enough,
He will eat it.

from *Young Scots Writing*

112

At that time there was neither nonexistence nor existence; neither the worlds nor the sky, nor anything that is beyond. What covered everything, and where, and for whose enjoyment? Was there water unfathomable and deep? Death was not there, nor immortality; no knowing of night or day. That One Thing breathed without air, by its own strength; apart from it, nothing existed. Darkness was there, wrapped in yet more darkness; undistinguished, all this was one water; the incipient lay covered by the void. That one Thing became creative by the power of its own contemplation . . . the gods are later than this creative activity; who knows, then from where this came into being? Where this creation came from, whether one supported it or not, He was supervising it from the highest Heaven, He indeed knows; or He knows not!

Rig Veda 10, 29

113

In AD 1309 an Aztec Indian inhabitant of what is now Mexico City was found guilty of burning charcoal in the city and polluting the air. He was ordered to be hanged for the offence.

Today, Mexico City has a carbon-monoxide level greater than metropolitan New York, a sulphur-dioxide level greater than that of London, and ten times the industrial contaminants of the industrialised Rhine River valley.

John McLaughlin

114

'Four buns, if you please,' said Sara. 'Those at a penny each.' The woman went to the window and put some in a paper bag. Sara noticed that she put in six. 'I said four, if you please', she explained, 'I have only fourpence.'

'I'll throw in two to make weight', said the woman. 'I dare say you can eat them sometime. Aren't you hungry?' A mist rose before Sara's eyes. 'Yes,' she answered, 'I am very hungry and I am much obliged to you for your kindness, and' – she was going to add – 'there is a child outside who is hungrier than I am.' But just at that moment two or three customers came in at once and each one seemed in a hurry, so she could only thank the woman again and go out. The beggar girl was still huddled up in the corner of the step. She looked frightful in her wet and dirty rags. She was staring straight before her with a stupid look of suffering, and Sara saw her suddenly draw the back of her roughened black hand across her eyes to rub away the tears which seemed to have surprised her by forcing their way from under the lids. Sara opened the paper bag and took out one of the hot buns, which had already warmed her own cold hands a little. 'See', she said, putting the bun in the ragged lap, 'this is nice and hot. Eat it, and you will not feel so hungry.' The child started and stared up at her, as if such sudden amazing good luck almost frightened her, then she snatched up the bun and began to cram it into her mouth with great wolfish bites.

Frances Hodgson Burnett

115

A wealthy family in England, many years ago, took their children for a holiday in the country. Their host toured over his estate for a weekend. The children went swimming in a pool. One of the boys began to drown, and the other boys screamed for help. The son of a gardener jumped in and rescued the helpless one. Later, the grateful parents asked the gardener what they could do for the youthful hero. The gardener said his son wanted to go to college. 'He wants to be a doctor', he said. The visitors shook hands on that. 'We'll be glad to pay his way through', they told him.

When Winston Churchill was stricken with pneumonia after the Teheran Conference, the King of England instructed that the best doctor be found to save the Prime Minister. The doctor turned out to be Dr

Fleming, the developer of penicillin. 'Rarely', said Churchill to Fleming, 'has one man owed his life twice to the same rescuer.' It was Fleming who saved Churchill in that pool.

Anon.

116

Laugh, laugh with joy. Lift up your hearts on high
For God is here, sharing our destiny.
We fight life's battles now with an ally.
Will you not hear the news, and laugh with me?

Be glad to give; be also glad to take
The gift of God, the giving and forgiving.
Give and accept, in joy that for our sake
The living God is here among the living.

John Ferguson

117

A gang of armed robbers are behind bars today after being tracked down by a group of East End schoolchildren.

The gang were jailed for a total of 20 years at the Old Bailey on Thursday for a £5,000 hold-up at an East London post office. Police are now planning to thank the children for helping to capture the bandits.

The children, aged about 10, became suspicious when they saw the gang dash from a getaway car. They followed the gang through the streets to the hideout and then ran to school to tell their teacher.

More than 200 police, some of them armed, and a helicopter were called to the hideout in Fife Road, Canning Town.

Detectives called for the gang to come out with their hands up, but finally burst in to arrest them and recover £5,000 stolen in the robbery.

Anon.

118

A big spider, which lived in the roof of an old house, decided to come and live a little lower down. So he spun a thread and came sliding down it and made a new web. He then began to catch flies and make himself fat and because he became fat he also became very stupid. He was very pleased with himself one day as he was walking round his web and he looked up and saw the thread going up in the air. 'What's the use of that?' he said and he broke it. Immediately, he went crashing down with his web to the floor beneath and killed himself.

Maurice Nassan

119

A 15-year-old Bedouin boy named Muhammed adh-Dhib, was searching for a stray goat in a desert region close to the Dead Sea, when he saw the opening of a small cave in a rocky cliff. He lazily threw a few stones through the hole and heard something break.

Thinking it might be hidden treasure, Muhammed ran back to camp and brought a friend, Ahmed Muhammed to the cave. They squeezed through the opening into the cave and found among pieces of broken pottery, a number of clay cylinders, 2 feet high.

Hoping for gold or precious stones the boys wrenched off the lids, but instead of the treasure they expected, they found only dark musty smelling lumps of material. They were 11 scrolls made of thin strips of sheep skin sewn together, and coated in gummy, decomposed leather.

More precious than gold, the Bible scrolls, hidden for nearly 1900 years, are the oldest Bible manuscripts ever found. While the boys families only received a few pounds from an Arab dealer, the world was enriched with a great religious treasure.

Anon

120

Dance over the mountains,
Leap over the sea.
Take a message to Manuel
That he belongs to me.

Shu-Ping is in China
Manuel is in Spain;
Round the world spin a girdle bright,
And round the world again.

Joy and peace are the girdle,
Love is the message we send;
You, Shu-Ping are my brother,
Manuel is my friend.

Bronya is sleeping in Poland,
Ranee's awake in Nepal;
Sunshine and shadow divide us,
But God watches over us all.

Dance over the mountains,
Leap over the sea.
Go and tell Lulu in Africa
That she belongs to me.

M.E. Rose

121

A tourist standing by Niagara Falls saw an eagle swoop upon a frozen lamb encased in a piece of floating ice. The eagle stood upon it and it drifted towards the rapids. Every now and then the eagle would proudly lift its head into the air to look around him, as much as to say: 'I am drifting on towards danger. I know what I am doing. I shall fly away and make good my escape before it is too late.'

When he reached the edge, he stopped, spread his powerful wings, and leaped for flight; but alas, while he was feeding on the carcase, his feet had frozen to its fleece. He leaped and shrieked, and beat upon the ice with his wings until he went over into the chasm and darkness below.

Anon.

122

After the teacher had told her class they could draw a picture of the Bible story she had told them, she went around to see what the children had done. She noticed that little Jenny hadn't drawn a Bible picture at all, so the teacher asked the child to tell the class about her picture.

'This is a car. The man in the front seat is God. The people in the back seat are Adam and Eve. God is driving them out of the Garden of Eden.'

Anon.

123

If you give a man a fish, he will eat once.
If you teach a man to fish, he will eat for the rest of his life.
If you are thinking a year ahead, plant a tree.
If you are thinking one hundred years ahead, educate the people.
By sowing seed, you will harvest once.
By planting a tree, you will harvest tenfold.
By educating the people, you will harvest one hundredfold.

Kuan-tzu (4th–3rd century BC)

INDEXES

Index of Hymns

Abbreviations

AM   *Hymns Ancient and Modern Revised* (William Clowes)
CH   *Celebration Hymnal,* volume I (Mayhew McCrimmon)
FH I   *Twentieth-Century Folk Hymnal* (Kevin Mayhew Ltd.), volume I
FH II   do., volume II
FH III   do., volume III
FH IV   do., volume IV
FP   *Folk Praise* (Kevin Mayhew Ltd.)
HON   *Hymns Old and New,* 2nd ed. (Kevin Mayhew Ltd.)
NL   *New Life* (Galliard)
NO   *New Orbit* (Galliard)
PL   *Praise the Lord,* revised ed. (Geoffrey Chapman)
SLW   *Sound of Living Waters* (also *Fresh Sounds,* Hodder and Stoughton)

First Line and References

All creatures of our God and King   AM 172, CH 4, HON 6, NL 43, NO 9, PL 261
All glory, praise and honour   AM 98, CH 8, HON 10, PL 184
All people that on earth   AM 166, CH 10, HON 14, NL 44, PL 11
All that I am   CH 11, FH I 49, FP 61
All the nations of the earth   CH 12, FH I 81, FP 62, HON 17
All things bright and beautiful   AM 442, CH 13, HON 18
All you who seek a comfort sure   AM 104, CH 15, PL 176
Amazing grace   CH 19, FH I 36, FP 73, HON 20, SLW 5
At the name of Jesus   AM 225, CH 28, FH II 81, HON 27, NL 136, SLW 45

Bind us together, Lord   FH IV 21, HON 33
Breathe on me, breath of God   AM 236, CH 37, HON 34, NL 86, PL 6
Bring, all you dear-bought nations   CH 38, HON 35

Christ be beside me   CH 41, FH II 13, FP 160, HON 39 (*see also* AM 162 (*part* II), PL 221a)

Lead us, heavenly Father, lead us   AM 311, CH 165, PL 112
Let all that is within me   CH 167, FH I 15, FP 159, HON 148, SLW 20
Lord, for tomorrow and its needs   CH 178, HON 156, PL 168
Lord, I want to be a Christian   SLW 36
Lord Jesus Christ   CH 179, FH I 100, FP 181, HON 159
Lord of all hopefulness   CH 181, HON 162, NL 54, NO 39, PL 288, SLW 44
Lord of the dance   CH 131, FH I 68, NL 28, NO 54, PL 92
Love divine, all loves excelling   AM 205, CH 184, HON 165, PL 113
Love is his word   CH 185, FH I 66, FP 107, HON 166, PL 75
Love is patient   FH IV 97
Love is something   NL 134, NO 14

Make me a channel of your peace   CH 189, FH I 35, FP 108, HON 167, SLW 97
May the long-time sun   FH IV 24
Mine eyes have seen the glory   CH 195, FH I 55, FP 214, HON 170
Morning has broken   CH 196, FH I 73, FP 196, HON 171, NL 79, SLW 9
Moses, I know you're the man   CH 197, FH I 98, HON 172
My God loves me   CH 205, FH II 24, FP 197, HON 176

No use knocking on the window   NL 19
Now thank we all our God   AM 379, CH 211, HON 180, NL 55, NO 33, PL 93
Now the green blade riseth   CH 53, FH II 14, HON 181, NL 36, PL 201

O Bread of heaven   CH 213, HON 183, PL 76
O Lord my God   CH 227, FH II 27, FP 8, HON 202
O sinner man   CH 229, FH I 22
Oh, the love of my Lord   CH 231, FH I 79, FP 81, HON 195
Oh when the saints   CH 232, FH I 91, FP 82
One more step along the world   NO 35

Peace is flowing like a river   CH 254, FH II 31, FP 221, HON 219, SLW 91
Peace, perfect peace   CH 257, FH I 2, FP 120, HON 220
Praise my soul, the king of heaven   AM 365, CH 260, HON 223, NL 58, PL 95
Praise to the Lord, the almighty   AM 382, CH 264, HON 226, NL 61, PL 14, SLW 11
Praise we our God with joy   CH 266, HON 228, PL 94

See amid the winter's snow   HON 236, PL 144

Suggested Recorded Music

The pop music industry is so vast and ever-changing that no complete list of useful titles would ever be possible. Here are some suggestions, listed under the headings SINGLES and LPs, including a few 'Golden Oldies'. Naturally, most of the singles can be found on LPs, but those listed have had a chart success and have appeared at least once in their own right. I have listed the singles according to possible assembly theme and the LPs according to artists.

Singles

Theme	Record	Artiste & Ref.no.
Aloneness	Half-way down the stairs	Muppets Pye 7N 45698
Bible	Deck of Cards	Max Bygraves Pye 7N 45276
Celebration	Grandma's party	Paul Nicholas RSO 2090 216
Charity	He ain't heavy, he's my brother	Hollies R 5806
Christ, figure of	Vincent	Don McLean UP 35359
Christian leadership	Bannerman	Blue Mink RZ 3034
Christmas	Gaudete	Steeleye Span CHS 2007
	When a child is born	Johnny Mathis CBS 4599
	Mary's boy child	Boney M K 11221
	Merry Christmas you suckers	Paddy Roberts Decca 11552
Communication	We don't talk anymore	Cliff Richard EMI 2975
Companionship	Two little boys	Rolf Harris DB 8630
Compromising	Rhinestone Cowboy	Glen Campbell CL 1582
Coping with evil	Rose Garden	Lynn Anderson CBS 5360 or New World RAK 111
Daily chores	Another day	Paul McCartney Apple R 5889
Death	Bright Eyes	Art Garfunkel CBS 6947
Dignity of individual	Woodstock	Matthews Southern Comfort UNS 526
Dignity of women	She	Charles Aznavour BAR 26
Easter	Morning has broken	Cat Stevens WIP 6121
Envy	The other man's grass	Petula Clark Pye 7N 17476
Exile	Rivers of Babylon	Boney M K 11120
Freedom	Fernando	Abba EPC 4036
	Sing a song of freedom	Cliff Richard DB 8835
God as friend	You've got a friend	James Taylor WB 16085
God in nature	All kinds of everything	Dana R 11054
God's people	Israelites	Desmond Dekker PYR 6058
Good Friday	Oh Happy Day	Edwin Hawkins singers Buddah 201 048
Grace	Amazing Grace	Judy Collins Elektra 2101 020
Happiness	Happiness	Ken Dodd Columbia DB 7325
Housing	Y.M.C.A.	Village People Mercury 6007 19

Human rights	We shall overcome	Joan Baez Fontana TF 564
Inspiration	Desiderata	Les Crane WB 16119
Jesus	Man from Nazareth	John Paul Jones RAK 107
Jesus as Lord	My Sweet Lord	George Harrison Apple R 5884
Joy of Freedom	Song of Joy	Miguel Rios A&M AMS 790
Listening to God	Turn your radio on	Ray Stevens CBS 7634
Loneliness	Eleanor Rigby	Beatles Parlophone R 5493
Love	All you need is love	Beatles Parlophone R 5620
	Love is like oxygen	Sweet Polydor POSP1
	Love lifted me	Ray Stevens CBS 8191
Mary	Lady Madonna	Beatles Parlophone R 5675
Materialism	Money, money, money	Abba EPC 4713
Near to God	Sailing	Rod Stewart WB 16600
Need for others	Help	The Beatles Parlophone R 5305
Needy	Streets of London	Ralph McTell K 14380
Peace	Give me love	George Harrison Apple R 5988
	Give peace a chance	John Lennon Apple 13
	Let there be peace on earth	Michael Ward Philips 6006 340
Prayer	Day by Day	Holly Sherwood Bell 1182
	A child's prayer	Hot Chocolate RAK 221
Providence	That's the way God planned it	Billy Preston Apple 12
	There but for fortune	Joan Baez Fontana TF 587
Questioning	There are more questions than answers	Johnny Nash CBS 8351
Race relations	Black and White	Greyhound Trojan TR 7820
Repentance	I don't know how to love him	Petula Clark Pye 7N 45112
Supreme Being	Spirit in the Sky	Norman Greenbaum RS 20885
Truth	What is truth?	Johnny Cash CBS 4934
Unity and Peace	I'd like to teach the world to sing	New Seekers Polydor 2058 184
Wonder of new born	Isn't she lovely	David Parton Pye 7N 45663
Work	Matchstalk men	Brian and Michael Pye 7N 46035
Young people	Everybody's talkin'	Nilsson RCA 1876

The sixty titles given above may often be used for themes other than those listed. For example, 'Sailing' by Rod Stewart could well be used for the theme 'Life's problems' or 'Temptation'.

LP's

ABBA   *Abba, the Album*   Epic 86052

One man, one woman   Communication in marriage
The name of the game   Our need for some one close who can help us to grow
Move one   The value and use of time

Abba Greatest Hits   Epic 69218

Fernando   Freedom
Nina pretty ballerina   Dignity of the individual
Ring Ring   Communication between people
Bang-a-Boomerang   Love given, returns

GLEN CAMPBELL   *Twenty Golden Greats*   Capital EMTV2

Both sides now   Balanced judgements
Reason to believe   Foundation for faith
Rhinestone Cowboy   Comprising one's integrity
The last thing on my mind   Breaking a relationship
Amazing Grace   God's grace

BOB DYLAN   *New Morning*   CBS 69001

New Morning   Easter
Father of Night   God the Father

GEORGE HARRISON
The Best of George Harrison   Parlophone PAS 1011

Here comes the sun   The feast of Easter
What is life   Truth will make you free
Think for yourself   Look around at the world
Something   We are people of worth
Give me love   The need for love; peace
Bangla Desh   The Third World
Taxman   Taxation
My Sweet Lord   Friendship with Christ

GODSPELL   *The Cast*   Bell records 1182

Prepare ye the way   Advent
Save the people   Advent
Turn back oh man   Lent
On the willows   Lent
Light of the World   Easter
Day by Day   Prayer

CAROLE KING   *Tapestry*   A&M records

Way over yonder   Easter
Beautiful   Easter

DON McLEAN   *Homeless Brother*   UAG 29646

The legend of Andrew McGrew   Personal identity
Sunshine life for me   Coping with worry
Winter has me in its grip   Loneliness
You have lived   Courage
Homeless Brother   The Needy

American Pie   UAS 29285

Vincent   Portrait of Christ
Crossroads   Need for reconciliation
Winterwood   Relationship with God transforms us
Empty chairs   Death and bereavement
The Grave   War; death of soldiers
Dreidel   Using life-time well

Prime Time   EMI NS 3011

Prime time   Street violence
The statue   Liberty; what happened to freedom?
Jump   Joy of life
The pattern is broken   Making sense of life's pattern
Colour TV blues   TV commercials; sign of rampant materialism
Building my body   Respect for the human body

JONI MITCHELL   *Ladies of the Canyon*   Reprise K 44085

The Circle Game   Inevitability of time
Woodstock   Dignity of individual

SIMON AND GARFUNKEL (all LPs have material)
Parsley, Sage, Rosemary and Thyme   CBS

7 o'clock News   Meaning of Christmas
Patterns   Pentecost
Cloudy   Pentecost

Wednesday morning 3am   CBS 63370

Sparrow   Lent
You can tell the world   Pentecost
Sounds of Silence   Man's inability to communicate

Bridge over troubled waters   CBS 63699

Bridge over troubled waters   Figure of salvation (Christ as mediator)
The Boxer   Growth to maturity
(These and others are gathered on *Simon and Garfunkel's greatest hits*, CBS 69003)

ROD STEWART   *Atlantic Crossing*   Warner Bros K 56151

It's not the spotlight   Christ the light of the World
Sailing   Coping with storms of life
Drift away   Young people searching for meaning

STEVIE WONDER   *Songs in the Key of Life*   EMI TMSP 6002

Have a talk with God   Prayer
Village Ghetto land   The deprived
Isn't she lovely   Wonder of the new born baby

It must be stressed that the above records are merely a few suggestions that might be used to enliven and illustrate an assembly.

Index to Readings

This has been compiled as an aid to those who wish to compile their own assembly using one or more of the 94 themes listed below – or who wish to enrich the existing assembly material with extra texts.

A reminder regarding the reference system:
– assembly references beginning with a letter (e.g. F50) refer to the first section of this book, the 'Prepared Assemblies';
– numerals only refer to the 'Alternative Assemblies';
– numerals above 100 refer to the 'Additional Readings' section.

Figures in brackets, e.g. (1), (2), refer to particular readings in an assembly.

See also the Contents pages at the beginning of the book.

Theme & Reference